Appalachia Mountain Folklore

Micheal Rivers

Schiffer Publishing Ltd®

4880 Lower Valley Road • Atglen, PA 19310

Other Schiffer Books by the Author:
Ghosts of the North Carolina Shores, 978-0-7643-3471-9, $14.99

Published by Schiffer Publishing, Ltd.
4880 Lower Valley Road
Atglen, PA 19310
Phone: (610) 593-1777; Fax: (610) 593-2002
E-mail: Info@schifferbooks.com

For the largest selection of fine reference books on this and related subjects, please
visit our website at:
www.schifferbooks.com.
You may also write for a free catalog.

This book may be purchased from the publisher.
Please try your bookstore first.

We are always looking for people to write books on new and related subjects. If you
have an idea for a book, please contact us at:
proposals@schifferbooks.com

Schiffer Books are available at special discounts for bulk purchases for sales promotions
or premiums. Special editions, including personalized covers, corporate imprints, and
excerpts can be created in large quantities for special needs. For more information
contact the publisher.

In Europe, Schiffer books are distributed by
Bushwood Books
6 Marksbury Ave.
Kew Gardens
Surrey TW9 4JF England
Phone: 44 (0) 20 8392 8585; Fax: 44 (0) 20 8392 9876
E-mail: info@bushwoodbooks.co.uk
Website: www.bushwoodbooks.co.uk

Copyright © 2012 by Micheal Rivers
Library of Congress Control Number: 2012947060

Designed by Stephanie Daugherty
Type set in NewBskvll BT/Gill Sans Std
ISBN: 978-0-7643-4006-2
Printed in the United States of America

For Joy, Laverne, and Bill...

Life is short, be good to yourself!

Contents

Foreword

When we think of folklore, many things come to mind. Some envision tales of ghosts and things that go bump in the night. Others dream of more whimsical tales of fairies and angels from above that have come to protect them from evil and the dangers of life. There are tales of laughter and sorrow. As varied as folklore can be, they all have one thing in common — all of them have yet to be proven as fact.

Regardless of who witnessed the event, the story (folklore) has been passed from generation to generation among friends, family, and strangers until the story has changed many times over. The tales all seem to hold the same quality of truth that keeps those hearing the stories spellbound for hours. These people long to witness an event themselves in an attempt to give their beliefs validity. After all, grandpa and grandma swore it was the truth!

Folklore will never die, whether it is in text or being passed along by the elders who hold their families dear to them. It goes hand-in-hand with protecting yourself as well as the things you learn from the stories about proper respect for the land and those around you. This also holds true for the spiritual side of your life.

Every race and nationality has its own folklore. Here in the mountains of Western North Carolina, you will find the tales of many cultures that came here to settle from other countries. Stories that emanate from Irish, the Scottish, and German ancestors abound. The others are the original people of this land, the Cherokee Indians, who taught the immigrants the stories of their people to try and help them as they settled this new land.

Thus, stories of legend and superstitions in these mountains are intertwined with the Cherokee and other tribes inhabiting the area through the years. The great history of these lands can never be forgotten, but be assured that the tales handed down through time involve everyone in every facet of their lives.

1

Jackson County

I n 1851, parts of Haywood County and Macon County, North Carolina, were taken and formed what is now Jackson County. It officially took its name from President Andrew Jackson, who served in office from 1829 to 1837. In 1799, the gold bug struck here before the California and Alaska gold fields were opened. Some of the former mines can still be found here. The county boasts fifteen townships threading their way to the Eastern Continental Divide. The majestic Blue Ridge Mountains, with its pristine waters, make it easy to envision the sights and sounds our ancestors once reveled in.

The grandest mystery of all is the pride of the Eastern Band Cherokee — Judaculla Rock. It is believed to be more than 3,000 years old and some say has powers beyond our knowledge. Steeped in legend and pride in their heritage, the citizens of Jackson County still hold true to the beliefs they were taught to cherish and live by. The outsider will call the tales of this land "folklore," but the people of this land know the truth is there...*if* you will take time to listen.

Written in Stone

Scientists, as well as the average man, have come to Jackson County for countless years. They have come to this place within the mountains of North Carolina to see an enigma of history written in stone. Judaculla Rock is without a doubt the best known petroglyph in the state of North Carolina. The symbols imprinted upon this soapstone boulder have never been deciphered, despite the best efforts of men with great experience and education.

In 1946, Cherokee Chief, Blythe, stated that he had deciphered the symbols carved into Judaculla rock. He said the writings were of the peace treaty between the Cherokee and Catawba Indians. This is still to be proven by archeologists who have studied the boulder of soapstone for generations. Many of the archeologists believe the writings to be as much as 3,000 years old.

The rock is covered with a series of circles, cupules, crosses, anthropomorphisms, and long grooved lines called power lines connecting the different symbols. Most peculiar of all is the seven-fingered handprint.

Judaculla Rock as it stands today. The fencing surrounding the rock was placed by archeologists working the site.

This photograph is a perfect example of the carvings that date back for more than three thousand years.

The late 1800s brought an ethnologist who documented the mystery behind Judaculla Rock. It was said to be a legend among the Cherokee and European settlers of a slant eyed giant who was responsible for this creation. According to the Cherokee, Judaculla was a mighty hunter who lived in the mountains nearby. He was known for being fierce, and ruled the Balsam Mountains like a mighty king.

There were many strange and wonderful tales told of his mother being a flashing comet and him being fathered by thunder. With his bow being the arc of heaven, he carried the arrows of the purist lightning. Men who claimed they knew of Judaculla swore he could drink whole streams dry with a single draught.

Judaculla was said to be able to step from one mountain to the next in a single stride. With a fearsome voice, he made the mountains rumble when he spoke. Yet all say he was horribly ugly; men turned from him in horror when they gazed upon his face. When the European Bible was translated for the Cherokee,

Sequoyah developed his syllabary and the word "Goliath" was changed to Judaculla.

It is difficult to think of any person being what Judaculla has been described to be: an enigma with seven fingers on his hands, as depicted in the great boulder itself. Did Judaculla have seven fingers on each hand? The pertroglyph says yes, and what is the meaning of the symbols dug deeply into the boulder that has lasted for centuries? For these things, we still seek the answers.

Legend states Judaculla carved the signs and symbols into the boulder using the fingernails of his huge hands. On the other side of the coin, legend also says he had a mate as mighty as himself.

Modern day Ufologists have another theory. With their studies and beliefs, they are convinced Judaculla was not from this planet. These men consider the signs and symbols to be a chart for fellow space travelers to read as a map of some sort. Hence, the power lines that connect the strange symbols marked upon the rock. Meanwhile, archeologists who have visited and studied the site believe the writings belong to the ancient Cherokee language long forgotten by those who live in the area now.

Tales are told both by the believer and the nonbeliever, but the truth is buried among those who first began the tale of Judaculla rock. Judaculla rock is designated as a sacred place for the Cherokee and should be respected as such if you should decide to visit a small piece of ancient history.

The Acheri

From the Eastern hemisphere stands a legend that can also be found in North American folklore. The Acheri is the same whether you hear it from the Hindu mythology, the American Indian, or the Europeans who settled here.

Living high in the top of the mountains, a young child, frail of body with pale gray skin, descends upon the young children of the small towns and communities to render human misery. She enjoys the havoc she reeks upon families and holds a particular satisfaction for her deeds.

The Acheri casts her shadow on the children, leaving them with a multitude of diseases and sickness for them to endure. She comes to the children by entering their villages dancing and singing while preying on their small bodies. It was also said that, at times, the older men and women of the villages heard the beat of a drum before their loved ones became ill. The very touch of her shadow brings respiratory diseases that spread through the village to others. The infection waits for nothing, occurring instantly with a vengeance.

It is believed by many people of other nations as well as the American Indians and early settlers that the Acheri was once an ill child. These people believe she died suffering terrible pain and infections within her body. As a result, they say, she seeks her revenge upon others.

The elders say if you hear her singing it heralds the coming of a deadly disease of which there is no cure and the death of a loved one is inevitable! However, there is believed to be some small protection against the Acheri. The color red is a universal color that provides protection for your children. Mothers and fathers adorn their children with shirts of red or sew a design of some sort into the cloth with red thread to protect them. Beads of red worn about the neck and wrist also give their children protection from the Acheri. The Acheri is a malevolent spirit and you must protect your children.

The belief in the Acheri is still strong among a small majority of people in the Appalachia. Here, they bring themselves to the local doctor for many medical reasons, as they still believe not only in the Acheri but other entities of foreboding as well. The believers come to modern science with a hope and a prayer that they can thwart the best efforts of the Acheri from taking the ones they love. Have we been successful in destroying the happiness of the Acheri? For the answer, you will have to ask the Acheri herself!

Song of the South

There is a strong belief among many that you should never make your home close to a cemetery. The fear of spirits who do not rest may come into your home. There are those who swear this to be truth, regardless of what others believe. Tales abound from those who have ventured to make their home close to a cemetery and wound up with more than they bargained for. This could be why the rent was so cheap?

In Jackson County, one such home lies close by a cemetery. The spirits who have made themselves at home here are not malicious, but they do make themselves known on a regular basis.

Song of the South Lane for all appearances is not an outstanding place. It is located within a few miles of a small town called Whittier, North Carolina. In the spring and summer months, it is a very peaceful and beautiful community of private homes. It lays snuggled neatly within a small valley surrounded by the Great Smoky Mountains.

Residents often sit on their decks and enjoy the pleasant evenings after a hard day's work watching the sun go down behind the mountains. The relative peace and quiet here at times is so pronounced you can hear your neighbors speaking hundreds of yards from your home.

Yet, with all of the pleasant things to see and good neighbors that are there when you need them, things are not what they seem to outsiders in this community. In one of the homes there are uninvited guests of the supernatural kind. In this home, one never knows what to expect or when something much out of the ordinary will occur.

May 2006 was an exciting time for Mike and his wife, Marie. They had purchased their home some months earlier while they were still living in the city of Chicago. When the time was right, they packed up their belongings and moved into their new home. Marie had never lived anywhere but Chicago and everything was new and different for her. She loved the peace and quiet as well as the beauty of the mountains surrounding them. She marveled at the clear Southern skies at night where a billion stars seemed to shine just for her.

As with any new home, changes have to be made. Mike began painting each and every room with the special colors she had picked out with great care. It was the shaping of a new life for the both of them. The couple soon encountered a surprise welcome to their new home late one morning shortly after they had moved in and were trying to get settled.

Marie had an errand to run and left Mike to his painting. He sat down before a window that looked out onto the gravel drive beside the house. As he painted carefully around the window, something made him look up at the driveway. He felt as if someone was staring at him. His eyes rested on an elderly woman, possibly in her seventies. She was dressed much as the older generation had dressed while doing housework. Her frock was a simple polka dot dress and brocade house slippers. Her grey hair was pulled tightly back into a bun resting on the back of her head. Her wrinkled face held no expression as she stared at him with coal black eyes. She stood staring and never spoke a word.

Mike smiled at her and said, "I'll be with you in just a second."

This Song of the South home is said to be haunted by spirits from a nearby cemetery.

Mike figured they were having their first visitor and his wife wasn't back yet. He glanced back to his paintbrush and laid it deftly on the top of the paint can to prevent the paint from getting on his carpeting. All of this had taken barely a few seconds. When he looked back for the old woman, she was no longer there. He looked to the left and right, but didn't see anyone!

Mike jumped to his feet and was going to go outside when he saw his wife drive into the yard. Mike asked her which way the old lady went. His wife looked at him as though he had lost his mind and told him nobody was in the yard.

Mike knew a woman of her age could not have disappeared so quickly, but she had. He told his wife what the woman had looked like, but she had seen absolutely nothing. It was later discovered there were no elderly people living in the neighborhood.

Time passed as Mike and Marie became engrossed in detailing their new home. The incident was forgotten for awhile. However, the old lady was only the beginning of the tales that would be told for as long as they live...

The days began to roll by and life seemed normal for the both of them. Marie was talking on the phone with a friend in Chicago. When the friend asked to speak to Mike, she suddenly heard the opening and closing of the back door. Footsteps could be heard plainly walking through the utility room towards her. She told their friend to hold on, as he had just walked in the door. She rose from her chair and stepped out of the little office...only to find that not a soul had entered the house.

Many incidents occurred following that day when footsteps would be heard coming into and across the utility room and then stop. At times it began at the hallway and went toward the back of the house as if leaving the utility room. The door was heard to open and close many times with no one there.

The occurrences within the home began to escalate. Mike lay on the sofa watching television one evening while his wife worked the late shift at the hospital. Suddenly he heard footsteps come through the utility room and enter the hallway.

Thinking she had returned early, he sat up and saw it wasn't Marie — yet the footsteps continued coming up the hallway, stopping within a few feet of him, at the end of the hall. This happened not just once, but on several occasions. Each time they would find the door securely locked from anyone coming in from the outside.

When all seemed quiet, a new and disturbing presence came to visit their home. Shadows darted across the rooms that could only be captured with the corner of your eye. You could never be sure about what was just seen, but there was never a doubt that *something* had crossed the room. Mike and Marie knew they were not alone in their home. They felt a presence near them often, but still could not see anything to warrant the feelings they were sensing.

Marie was a skeptic to say the least. However, the things that were happening to her as well as her husband were slowly but surely dissolving all of her doubts about the supernatural.

One afternoon the couple returned home after a drive through the mountains...only to find another mystery added to the already mounting evidence of paranormal activity. They opened the utility room door and stepped through the doorway. The sound that reached their ears was loud. It was the crashing of an antique plate hitting the floor of the kitchen. The plate was placed upon a ledge on top of the cabinets. It was virtually impossible for the plate to fall from its resting place! Yet the plate, along with its tripod, had gone over the ledge, hitting the stove hard enough to chip gouges into the enamel. The plate lay in the kitchen floor face down without a scratch on it anywhere. Antique porcelain shatters easily, so how did a fragile piece of history fall from a height of eight feet without any damage?

Some days later Marie and her husband lay in bed talking late one night and to their surprise something, for want of a better word, came into their bedroom and sat on the bed at her husband's feet. It felt like the weight of a real human being. She listened as her husband told her what was happening. As he lay in bed with her, the entity changed position and lay

The ottoman was moved so the antique plate could be seen. It fell eight feet to the floor and was discovered thirteen feet from its original position into an adjoining room beneath the ottoman. Note: The plate is delicate porcelain and square. The plate cannot roll.

snuggled against his back, rubbing his hair as gently as a lover in the night. A ghostly hand then reached over and began to stroke his forearm gently as Mike and Marie talked about what was happening. Marie was finding all of this a little hard to believe until she looked at her husband's arm. The corner of the pillow — a half inch from his forearm — was moving up and down as if an unseen thumb was moving in unison with the rubbing of his forearm. This ghostly caress lasted for a few minutes.

Mike had felt the weight of someone sit at the end of the bed twice before, but this was the first time he had been touched by an unseen entity! It wouldn't be the last time either!

Evenings were usually a peaceful time in this valley, but for this home it could be a challenge for your own sanity. Marie stood by the end of the kitchen island where the two of them often ate their evening meal. Mike had retired to the back office and she was alone. Suddenly the figure of a man dressed in a red and beige plaid shirt scrambled on all fours down their hall before her very eyes. He disappeared almost as quickly as he had been seen. Though she could see through the figure, he was very close to being as solid as you or me. He wore a wide black belt and old style denim trousers. His hair was long and coal black, cut in what was described as "ragged" or an unkempt home cut. All of the colors of his clothing and the man himself were easily distinguishable to her. Mike was very close in the other room and saw nothing. She called out to him, but he was too late to see anything. She was visibly shaken from her experience.

There never seemed to be anything to fear when the unexplainable happened in their home. The couple took all these things in stride and with more than a little wonderment. Months went by and they had become accustomed to the strange happenings. Two years had passed when Marie invited a close friend and her husband to come visit them. Kathy had been Marie's best friend for more years than either of them wanted to admit and shared each other's life like sisters. The time came for Mike and Marie to gather their friends at the airport in Asheville, an hour from their mountain home. It was a joyous occasion for the two of them to see each other again. While on the trip home, Mike jokingly told Kathy if she happened to see anything out of the ordinary not to pay any attention to it. They all laughed and she agreed. The visit was pleasant and all concerned really enjoyed themselves immensely until the second morning of the visit.

Kathy and her husband lay talking in bed by the soft light of the rising sun. The guest room was all anyone could have asked for and the bed was heaven for them. A soft sound came from the door of the room causing them both to turn their attention to the entry. It was as if someone was coming in to visit them. The doorknob turned slowly and then the door opened almost twelve inches. They waited patiently, but no one ever came into the room. Instead the door closed on its own accord and latched shut.

Later that morning Kathy asked if either Mike or Marie had started to visit them that morning. Much to Kathy's surprise, both Mike and Marie said they had been asleep at the other end of the house when their guest's door opened on its own accord. The door that opened on its own has to be pulled solidly to latch itself securely!

Sometime after this, a photograph was taken showing a heavy vapor that appeared by the arch of the kitchen and moved down the hall into the back office. That same night, Mike went to the back door next to the office to check if it had been locked for the night. A feeling of dread bordering on fear crept into him and he felt as if he could not get back to his bedroom fast enough. This happened only once and never again. He felt as if he was intruding on someone's privacy.

A pleasant winter's evening brought to them yet another unexplained happening. Marie lay sleeping peacefully next to her husband when she was suddenly awakened from her sleep by the overpowering scent of Orange Blossom perfume. She jumped from her bed because the scent was really strong in the room. She was filled with anger. She leaned closer and smelled her husband as he slept and found the scent was not coming from him, much to her relief. The scent finally faded and she climbed back into bed and returned to sleep.

Many days later, digging into a kitchen drawer Marie was looking for a certain spatula she used for icing cakes. She knew it was in this drawer and yet she could not find it. It was not to be found anywhere! Instantly, Mike got the blame for the disappearance of the spatula. They both looked everywhere for it, but it was not to be found. The next day they were standing by the drawer where the spatula normally was placed and talked about where it could be. They both emptied the drawer and then replaced the items. The spatula was not to be found. Mike opened the drawer to get another utensil — and there lay the icing spatula on top of all the others. It was another case of items reappearing after they were missing just a day earlier.

At times life can take a turn for the worse and your family is your best friend. They are usually there to help when you need it most. Mike invited one of their children to come and stay with them until he could decide what he would like to do with his life. It was a chance for them to help one of their children get back on their feet. The son stayed for a few months and decided it was time for him to move to a place of his own. Something refused to let him sleep at times while he was in the guest room. There were strange noises and other things he refused to talk about. Something about the room was deeply disturbing to him. He announced he would never sleep in the room again.

Voices in the night, laughter, whispers, and being touched by someone who isn't there is all part of Mike and Marie's home. It has been quiet lately here in the valley, but for how long?

The House on the Hill

A re there spirits who stay just to protect and care for the living? People may not agree on this point, yet there are times when the evidence will say otherwise. A home is a living thing that breeds love and life for those who live there. If a house is left empty and nobody to care for it, the spirit of the house will die just as a person eventually does.

There are few things more exciting, or precious, than two people in love. They see a life they will build for themselves and their children. Through the best of life and the times that will surely test them, they endure all that comes their way. They do these things bound by an undying love for each other.

When the nuptials are over and the flowers have faded, it is time for them to begin the life they have planned for so long. Soon, these young couples decide its time for them to find just the right home to build their dreams and raise a family. This is not always an easy task. Many times it is not the price of the house that makes them refuse certain places. It has to be suitable for both of them. The right amount of bedrooms, the shed out back, the lighting in the kitchen... Hundreds of things must be decided before just the right place enters their lives.

This was once the home of Charmie and Scott Cooper. Charmie still inhabits the house, protecting the babies of the new owners.

Mark and his new bride made their way through the long listing of houses not finding exactly the new home that would satisfy them both. Discouraged, they came to believe that the perfect house for them wasn't there, yet the time for waiting became shorter than they thought. A family member told them of a house they felt would be very nice for them. The best part was the price. No, the house was not cheap nor was it in complete disrepair, but it had been empty for two years before they purchased the house and began to move in.

The house was a very quaint stone front cottage in a very good location. It was convenient to everything the town of Sylva, North Carolina, had to offer. It was also very convenient to their church and friends.

This home seemed to hold everything they needed and more. They began to change some things in the home to make it their own. It was a happy time for them and then they were blessed with children. Two beautiful children, a blessing indeed!

They grew with their home and the community. Each Sunday they attended church services and had good times with their friends whenever possible. Life was good!

However, soon after the first child was born, Mark and his wife started to hear noises in their home. It was not unusual to hear someone walking up the stairs who could not be seen. One afternoon Mark's wife and her best friend heard the sound of a woman's laughter coming from the kitchen. They left the living room and went into the kitchen to see who was there. The kitchen was empty. On several occasions someone in the house would hear the laughter of a woman who was not to be found.

Mark sat watching television in the living room while spending time with his family. He rose from his chair and made his way to the kitchen to get himself something to drink. Rounding the corner, he was assaulted by the pungent smell of cigarette smoke. It was a very strong smell. There was nobody in the house who smokes and nobody had been in the house but Mark and his family.

Sounds of footsteps echoed through their home regularly from a person or persons who could never be seen by them. The entity did not just confine his activities to Mark and his wife. The sounds and smells were introduced to others as well, including the local minister who was house-sitting for them. These sounds were very abrupt and obvious to the minister, for he knew he was alone in the house. Hearing these unexplained sounds, he abandoned his post and returned to his home. The minister had smelled the cigarette smoke also, but he paid little heed to it. The footsteps of an unknown origin were more than he wanted to endure.

Mark's wife soon began to notice her child was staring at something unseen by the large front window in her living room. It was a mere few feet from the window itself and looking back toward the stairs. The child would sit and grin, sometimes laughing at what appeared to be nothing. This worried her to no end and she was quick to inform her husband of what was happening. Soon he too began to notice the child's actions. However, the child was not to be denied of his newfound, invisible friend. At times he became irritable if he was removed from where he could see the area he watched so fervently.

Mark soon delved into the history of the house and became convinced his family was being visited by the former owner. Her name was Charmie.

Charmie was known to have loved children. Mark and his wife were soon to discover that the spot his son watched was the very spot Charmie had sat for so many years in her favorite chair. This also convinced them their visitor was none other than Charmie.

The question still remained concerning the smell of cigarette smoke in the house. Those who knew Charmie swore that she never smoked! The footsteps that reverberated throughout the house were also too heavy to have been a woman. The obvious answer to them was Charmie's husband, Scott. He was known to smoke and, being a man, his footfall would have been much heavier than a woman's. Both Charmie and Scott had died many years ago.

Mark and his wife became convinced Charmie was helping them keep the child safe. The child grew to be almost two years of age when Mark noticed the house had quieted down to almost nothing. They had not seen or heard any activity in the house since the child had become old enough to walk and speak clearly for himself.

The family was once again blessed with another child and immediately the house became active once more. The spirits were now louder and bolder than ever before. This child also would gaze for long periods of time at the place Charmie once sat.

While cleaning her home, Mark's wife and oldest son were in the addition, which is the master bedroom. In the corner by the closet is a large pile of toys belonging to the boys. Without hesitation, her son pointed to a corner and asked his mother, "What is that?" She could see nothing and yet he insisted there was something there. Due to his young age, he was unable to explain what he was seeing. It was not long in coming before the father had the same experience with his son. Neither of the parents were able to see anything. The child's attention was drawn to the corner of the room each time he entered.

The sounds heightened in intensity: sounds of running back and forth in the bedroom over the living room were heard very clearly over the volume of the television being played downstairs. There was nobody else in the home at the time but Mark and his family downstairs.

Weekends are a time for a gathering of friends and fun times. The minister had children of his own and they all enjoyed visiting with Mark's family. The minister drove up the driveway approaching the house carefully trying to avoid any stray toys that may be in the drive. He had a son he lovingly nicknamed "Tater"; Tater pointed toward the second floor window and asked his father who the old woman was standing in the window. The minister saw nothing, yet the child was able to describe an old woman who fit the description of Charmie perfectly. He had never seen a picture of Charmie in his young life. Much to the minister's surprise, the house was empty at the time of the sighting. Mark and his family were all outside waiting for them to arrive.

Not all of the ghostly happenings could be placed on Charmie or Scott, though. Items would come up missing when they were in their possession just seconds before. At times they would reappear, but most of the time they were gone forever. Mark's wife prepared herself to go out shopping for a few things she needed for the babies as well as herself. She was sitting at the computer desk when her cell phone began to show the words "mom calling," but no ring. Regardless of what she tried, she was unable to remove the message. Removing the battery should have cleared the phone of the message, but this was of no avail. The message refused to go away or be erased.

Recently, Mark had a yard sale. Among the items he sold was the former furniture dipping equipment in the garage that belonged to Scott. Strange happenings are still the norm in his home; the minister relayed the incident of Mark witnessing the opening of the garage door by unseen hands.

It would seem Charmie and Scott have dedicated themselves to protecting the children of Mark and his beloved family.

A Plea for Help

A mile or so from the town of Dillsboro in Jackson County is the intersection leading to Dick's Creek. Within this fine little community, a legend still rings through the valley and hills

The curve where Suzy and her son lost their lives and are seen on the road by modern day witnesses.

surrounding the residents there. The road winds its way up into the community surrounded by the mountains, its sharp turns and twists warning you very quickly to slow down and take your time in your travels.

During the early 1800s, this stretch of woodland lined road was unpaved. In the summer, the wheels of the wagons and buggies filled the air with dust. In the winter, the mud was thick and made travel difficult for the residents of the mountain.

A legend continues today about a school teacher named Suzy who lost her life on Dick's Creek. The tale was told to Beth by her great-grandfather when she was just a child. Accounts of this horrible accident vary according to the witness. The teacher, along with her child, was traveling home in her horse-drawn buggy on a warm August evening. She seemed to be in a hurry. The reason for the rush has been lost through time, but the story remains. As she came to a sharp turn in the road, she lost control of the buggy, causing it, and the horse, to run off the side of the mountain.

The child was severely injured and she feared the worst for him if she didn't get help and soon, so Suzy climbed from the watery ravine up the side of the mountain and found her way back onto the dirt road. It was actually her spirit that made its way back onto the road because residents found her and her son dead at the bottom of the ravine. They had been killed instantly when the buggy rolled over on them. The first people on the scene swore they saw her standing by the road...only to disappear when they approached the drop-off where she had lost control.

Years have passed and yet Suzy has still managed to make herself known to travelers. The strangers would be traveling up the road on the way to visit other people in the community. A woman walking the road heading up into the hollow could be seen as plainly as a normal person. They would stop and ask her if she needed a ride up the mountain. Suzy would tell them she had been in an accident and needed to get home for help. The travelers never realized when she left the vehicle. They would turn to continue their conversation and Suzy would no longer be

The drop off from the side of the curve as seen today.

riding with them. She spoke not in a ghostly whisper nor did she have the usual wispy appearance. No distinct smell accompanied her and she did not fear looking into the eyes of those she chose to ride with.

Some have sworn they have seen the child crawling up the side of the mountain on the far side of the creek, but these tales are very few and far from the original tale of the accident. Of the many who have reported helping Suzy, the story always varies, but only slightly. The difference is usually in the length of time Suzy has accompanied them along the road. The stories seldom tell of what Suzy was wearing or her condition at the time she is helped in her hour of distress.

If this tale is true, it is our hope that Suzy is someday able to get the help she is looking for so she may rest in peace.

Gold for the Greedy

In 1799, gold was discovered in North Carolina. The gold bug struck as mightily here as it did in the gold fields of Alaska and California. Reaching into the mountains, people by the score came to dig and mine for the gold that would make all their dreams come true. Some of the former mines can still be found here and visitors from other lands come yearly just to catch a glimpse of the mineral that drove men mad with greed.

The North Carolina Gold Rush was the first in the United States, soon to be followed by the state of Georgia. Jackson County was not immune to the gold fever. Once gold was found here, the towns, such as Sylva, began to flourish. Stores, a doctor's office, and a place to worship were built to supply the miners, as well as the sudden growth of people and families looking for ways to take advantage of the new discovery. Opportunity only knocks once and they all answered the call. Expert miners were called in from countries such as England, Scotland, Wales, and Germany. The Cornish miners were very superstitious and refused to come to America without their families. English-speaking, the Cornish had little or no trouble settling in with the surrounding communities.

This is a prime example of a sluice. This one is used for water to operate a mill. A sluice much like this was also used for the mining of gold.

All of these men and women from other countries left their mark upon the mountains of North Carolina and their customs still stand strong here.

A tale is told of two men from Scotland who ventured into the mountains to make their fortune in gold. The land they purchased was not easy to access. The two men decided they would work their claim during the week and return to their homes on the weekends. Their claim was kept as quiet as possible for fear of others wanting to be in on their discovery should they strike it rich. In their homeland, they had worked the coal mines as well as the gold fields in search of a better life for themselves and their families. They were no strangers to the rigors of hard work.

Somewhere circa 1804 the two men struck a vein of some of the finest gold in North Carolina. They worked the vein feverishly trying to gather as much of the gold as they possibly could before having to return home again. A change in their routine would certainly alarm others as to their discovery. When the time arrived for them to go home, they decided to bury their gold instead of taking it with them. Once a place they felt was secure was found, they buried their gold during the night and left early the next morning for home.

The two men never let their family know of their new discovery, even though the news was all but impossible to keep to themselves. They had made a pact that neither of them would tell of the discovery until the time was right.

It was agreed the men would return to their mine on schedule so as not to be noticed. The gold they had buried was still as they had left it and both men were satisfied of its safety. Just as history would be quick to tell us, North Carolina and its gold fields were no strangers to thieves and robbers. Con men, with their own nefarious agendas, were plentiful in places such as this. The Scots feared for their newfound fortune and had no desire to lose the gold or their lives.

A fortune in gold steadily grew as the days drew on. Each night their hoard of precious metal would be safely tucked away until they would need it. Subtly at first, but then climbing at an alarming rate, the gold began to come between the two friends. Arguments came close to actual fights and mistrust for each other was gaining momentum. They stayed within each other's sight at all times for fear of one taking more than his share.

Their next trip home the two men agreed to take a small amount of the gold with them. There were bills to be paid and tiny mouths to feed in their absence. Once they arrived home, it was soon discovered strangers had been asking about their claim. This worried them to no end. Questions arose concerning their safety. Yet they had no choice but to return because their entire fortune still lay buried close to the mine. It was decided they would start keeping their guns close to them. To take a chance could mean the price of losing their life.

As the weeks passed, the gold amassed and they discovered it could not all be taken home in one trip. It weighed much more than they or their animals could carry, so the Scots brought home enough gold to raise eyebrows in the small town. Strangers began to ask questions they were not obliged to answer for any man. Veiled threats came to them and their families for not sharing in their good fortune. The men knew they had waited too long to move their gold. Trust between the two men was all but gone!

Winter was showing its first signs of moving in. The cold was almost more than they could bear. In a fit of rage over how to handle their fortune, one of the Scots struck his friend with the sharp edge of a shovel, almost decapitating him. Within minutes, he was dead. Explaining his actions to the law would be difficult, but he had a story he felt would pass inspection by anyone. Without a second thought, he packed his bag with all the gold he could carry and set off down the mountain in the dead of night. He made four trips on that night. Each trip his bags were laden with the gold they had worked so hard for. The partner had no intention of sharing any of the gold with his friend's family. The gold was buried further down the mountain close to the riverbed where nobody would ever find it.

On his fourth trip back to the camp, he saw the body of his friend still laying in the pool of fresh blood as he had left him. He would stick to his story of his partner's attempt to kill him for the gold and none would be the wiser. In his pack, he carried just enough gold to verify his story and no more. The rest of the hoard would stay hidden until he had time to move away from the little town for a better life. However, this was not to be!

For the last time, the Scot stepped into the night, never knowing the fate awaiting him. Slowly through the darkness, he made his way down through the wooded hillside of the mountain. By his side he carried his rifle for protection. His eyes were keen and he listened intently to every noise he heard in the woods around him. With every step, he began to hear more sounds all around him. Fear crept into his soul and he brought his rifle to the ready. Just ahead of him in the middle of the trail a patch of mist began to form. He paid little attention to this until he was almost standing within its bounds.

He heard the voice of his dead partner whispering to him. The voice never wavered as it warned him of dangers ahead of him. He traveled on ignoring the voice of a dead man he had left behind. Strangers who had been trying to find their claim had discovered the trail the Scots had been using. Within minutes of hearing his friend's voice, the strangers pounced on the Scot, beating him with no mercy. They robbed him of the gold he carried and the Scot would not tell where their claim lay in the hills. The robbers killed the Scot, so there would not be a witness to their deed.

Unfortunately for them, the robbers were soon caught and confessed to their heinous crime. During their confession, the robbers told the story the Scot had relayed to them. He told them he was warned by his dead partner they were coming for him. The jury also found them guilty of killing the man that was found in the gold camp belonging to the Scots. They claimed no knowledge of where the camp was, but the verdict was in. They paid with their own lives for the robbery and murder of two men.

The tale of a man who appears to have been beaten walked the banks of the river for dozens of years. He has not been sighted since the early 1900s. Was this the ghost of the Scot? The thought of him returning for his gold is always the possibility. The gold buried by the banks of the river has never been found and the tale of the Scots is buried in the past.

Ride with You

The Cherokee reservation is a place of mystery as well as a long history. There are tales to entice the mind, legends with an endless life, and events that cannot be denied! This is a land of magic and mystery with no bounds. There are road signs leading you to the homes of the Cherokee written in their own language (as well as in English). Traditions are strong and family is of the greatest priority.

Traveling on the roads of the reservation, visitors pass shops, a museum, and restaurants looking for souvenirs you cannot find in other places. The sights and sounds of the music can be very exciting. Those who spend their lives here are well aware of one road more than any other. Big Cove is an approximately twelve-mile road that ends at what is known as the loop. It begins close

Monument to greet visitors to the Cherokee Reservation.

The sign welcoming you to Big Cove and the people of Raven Rock.

to the intersection of Acquoni Road and Highway 441. Shops once belonging to Chief Henry and others are here for all to see. The Cherokee storytellers and dancers are just two of the things you will find here by the clear, rolling waters of the reservation.

There is a time in the evening drivers on this road try to avoid if possible. It is a very unnerving experience when you are driving alone and suddenly you have a passenger riding with you — especially if the passenger is not of this world! This is not an ordinary or new event. This has been happening long before the first automobile ever graced the roads of the Big Cove. Chief Henry spoke of this happening when he was a small child in the 1930s.

The cool of the evening was fast approaching. Henry and his father were riding a well-worn cart being pulled by a government mule. The mule had been awarded to them for the use of farming, but it was rarely used for anything except to ride or pull the cart. Henry had traveled into Sylva to get some supplies his father needed, but the Bryson City suppliers did not have what he had wanted. The trip was long and they left home before the sun shone in the early morning sky. Finishing his business, the pair had stayed in Sylva, making some stops along the way, for too long. Henry's father pushed the mule to move faster, but to no avail. It seemed important to him that they reach their home before darkness fell.

In the manner of most children, Henry wanted to know why his father would never travel Big Cove Road at night. Some days later while he and his father sat on the porch talking, his father told him a puzzling story.

"Some years back I was talking with some of the other men at the store just down the road. There was some talk about an old man they used to see for many years that walked everywhere he went. The men I was talking with are mostly pretty old and not known to lie.

"The old man died in the winter of 1920, but the story doesn't end there. It seems many people have seen him walking down the road headed for the reservation. A few more years passed and he was seen no more. His spirit did not walk the road as it did before. Everybody saw this as a good thing. They figured his spirit was at rest.

"Soon the times changed. One of the men was coming home just after dark and he thought he was alone in his cart. A strange smell came to him and he turned to look what had caused it. It was a strange smell like the dirt of the mountain when it is wet in summer. When he turned, there was the old man riding with him. He had known the man for too long not to recognize him. He was not afraid of the old man's spirit, but he did not want to ride with him either. The old man's spirit did not speak. He just looked ahead and nodded often.

Before anything could be done, the old man's spirit vanished in the mist. The man thought maybe he had dreamed of the old man's spirit, but he had not. The seat was wet where the old man had sat. This happened to many people and soon we stopped riding the road after dusk."

Henry asked his father if he had ever seen the spirit of the old man, but received no answer. There are those who still do not ride

The road where the unknown rider is said to have been encountered over the years. A strange glowing ball of light was observed here while the photographs for this book were being taken.

Big Cove Road at certain times of the evening, even today. The fear of having the spirit of the old man as a rider is not a chance they wish to take. Some have said they have experienced the spirit riding with them. Accordingly, he will appear on the seat next to them and leave when he wants. He never speaks, but he does let you know what you have witnessed is not a dream. The front seat of modern automobiles was left wet with the lingering smell of damp earth in the air about you.

The spirit world is still a place where we are strangers. Why and when a spirit comes back to visit with us is another question we are not able to answer.

A Tale of Two Floors

There are many hospitals located in the mountains of Western North Carolina, and one stands out among the rest. Spirits roam these halls and rooms with little regard for the living walking among them. Some are former patients while others are former employees. There have been changes to the building over the years that may seem drastic in some cases. It is a fact the changes were necessary and made their jobs more efficient. Location is everything. In this hospital, the morgue is located directly across from the emergency room. It is also adjoining the kitchen where the food for the entire hospital is prepared daily.

The number of people who die in hospitals across the nation is staggering. The reasons for their death range anywhere from simple old age (natural death) to complications from disease or surgery. Among these are said to be souls who do not rest. Beliefs are variable on this subject, but the basis is always the same: they all seem to be looking for something they are unable to find. Are they trying to locate a loved one or the way out of the hospital to go home?

This Western North Carolina hospital stands alone among these mountains, but the strange happenings are anything but ordinary. There is a corridor that runs alongside the cafeteria with a small door at each end of the dining area. The first door has shelved carts in which those who have eaten can place their trays for cleaning. Several employees of the kitchen staff have remarked of seeing someone walking beside them as they swapped carts and were pushing them back to the kitchen. It was so obvious that they sometimes stopped to assure themselves they were not getting ready to hit someone with the cart.

A former employee was released from her duties as a supervisor after many years. To say she was upset would not justify her actions when she was told she was no longer needed. Other employees stated this former supervisor had an outrageous temper when crossed. The kitchen staff had many problems after she passed from this world. It would seem the supervisor returned to get her revenge on the staff. A remark was made toward her as two employees were crossing the kitchen, and a large meat fork flew through the air missing the new supervisor and a security guard, hitting the staff member in the back. When the staff member walked by the shelving, items fell from them or were thrown at her. All of this happened before more than one witness. For as long as the employee kept her job she was never safe from objects falling or being thrown at her from an unknown source.

At times security would be asked to go to the kitchen after hours and get ice cream or frozen dinners for late arrivals. Security guards would go down to the kitchen and return with the food. However, this did not last for long. They started placing frozen dinners on the different floors, along with milk and desserts, so they would not have to enter the kitchen.

The security guards started to fear the kitchen. Not the kitchen per se, but what was residing in there. Disembodied voices were heard and they always had a feeling of someone being very close to them while getting what they needed. The huge pots and pans would start to swing on their hooks, but there was no air circulating for this to happen. The weight alone of these pots and pans would forbid it from happening. Regardless, the pots and pans would all start to swing on their hooks at the same time and seem to gather momentum.

The second floor of this facility is no stranger to visions of patients who are no longer with them. A nurse of almost thirty years was party to a frequent sighting of one of her former patients. This sighting was not hers exclusively. Others witnessed the gentleman as well. The door of his former room was heard to open and close on its own. The sound of bedroom shoes on cement were heard to shuffle their way down to the elevator located across from the nurse's station. The light came on summoning the elevator. On several occasions the spirit was made known to them. There was no mistaking who the patient was!

It would only travel to the first and second floors when the apparition made his nightly rides. The elevator sometimes would travel this way for hours. When it was over, the footsteps could be heard returning to the room. Hospital maintenance never found a problem with the operation of the elevator and could not explain how the elevator could be summoned to this floor without someone to physically push the call button.

Strange events are not always experienced in the dead of night, though. In this facility of healing, former employees have been seen rounding corners going down another hallway. This was not possible because the former employee had been dead for many years. They were dressed just as they had been when they were on duty. One employee had only been deceased for two weeks when a prominent surgeon spoke to him in the hallway leading to the room that was used to perform MRI testing. He learned later in the day that the man he saw was deceased.

When things have gone very quiet and the morgue is not in use, cooks entering at 4 a.m. have heard unusual sounds from there through the walls of their walk-in freezer. They find out quickly there is no one in the morgue and it is securely locked. After a year or so they stopped questioning what they heard and carried out their duties as if everything is as it should be.

Now, you are no doubt questioning what this has to do with folklore. It has everything to do with folklore. It is believed when a soul is unhappy and cannot find peace it will make itself known to those around them. A sudden death, the loss of your loved ones, leaving your home and passing in a strange place...these can all bring on an earnest desire to return where the spirit feels he belongs. As for those who return to where they work, I sincerely hope it was for the love of their job and friends they miss.

2

Swain County

Swain County, North Carolina, is the home of the Nantahala River. This is a winding river paradise for whitewater rafters worldwide. The pristine beauty of the surrounding forests and mountains brings peace to even the most troubled souls. It was formed in 1871 from parts of Jackson and Macon counties.

Tales of ghosts and spirits are no stranger here. The history of Swain County is long and bountiful. The Catawba, Cherokee, and White settlers left their mark upon these hills by passing on their beliefs and ways of life. Ancient cemeteries, well hidden from view, dot the mountains. Once a year the ancestors of one town gather lakeside to be able to travel to the cemetery of their loved ones. Where is this town, you ask — at the bottom of Fontana Lake.

The Spirit of Father

L illie was tall for her age. At nine years old, you would have guessed her to be much older than she actually was. She had a knack for putting you at ease when she was near you. It was almost as if you had known her all of your life. She lived on the Cherokee reservation in North Carolina; everyone knew her and her family. She was usually seen on her way to visit a friend.

She grew up walking through the woods and over the mountains with her father and mother. She learned the ways of nature, loving the sight of everything around her. Her family elders taught her the wonders of natural remedies she could use to cure colds or injuries to herself and others. Lillie did not neglect the spiritual side of her life as she learned the way of her people. There was never a time in her life that she was not thankful for what was given to her. She felt blessed in every way.

At times it is hard for a child to judge time. Lillie always did her very best to adhere to her parent's wishes. After all, the punishment could possibly cause a sore bottom for not obeying. Lillie understood the things they told her were for her own protection and a way to learn the ways of the world.

Many times Lillie was allowed to cross the mountain on the reservation to go and visit other families. It was the 1940s and America was at war, but this was a far cry from her home and did not seem to affect her as it did her friends. She would visit families who had received the telegram concerning a loved one lost to battle. Though all of this was still beyond her tender age of understanding, she understood sadness and loss all too well and tried her best to comfort those she felt in need.

In listening to the teachings of her family, her father often told her he would always be with her no matter where she was. She believed in what he told her and yet she had little understanding how she could be in one place and he another while still being with her. Lillie was soon to learn he spoke the truth when he assured her safety.

A warm summer day brought a smile to Lillie's face as she stood looking toward the mountaintop where her best friend lived.

With little forethought, she raced back to her house and begged permission to go and visit her friend for the day. Her mother smiled and cupped her little chin in her hand and she looked into her eyes. "Yes, you can go and visit for the day, but you must be home by dark."

This bit of news was very exciting. Darkness would not fall until nine o'clock, which meant she would be able to eat supper with her dear friend and still be home on time. Elated, Lillie raced out the front door and across the meadow.

Every moment of the day was filled with excitement for the two friends. They fished in the river for trout and caught enough for everyone to enjoy. They spoke of their dreams for the future as well as who was the cutest boy in the village, all attributes of a young flower in blossom. When it came time for Lillie to leave, she realized she had tarried on too long at her friend's and darkness would be full upon her before she got home. The way of the mountain is long and she prayed she would remember the path well.

Lillie had been following the path for a full two hours when she suddenly realized it no longer looked familiar to her. She stopped in her tracks and gazed around her. Something was amiss. The path was unclear and a heavy fog was fast moving among the trees distorting everything in her sight.

A small pang of fear pierced her heart. Lillie knew the mountain could become very treacherous when a fog settled in. Over the years she had heard the tales of those who fell off the side of the mountain while trying to navigate through the fog. She ventured a few more feet ahead and sat down on an old stump wondering what to do. It was then she heard her father call her name. Lillie looked up to see a man standing some feet from her holding a lantern. His face was obscured by the rim of fog, but it was surely her father's voice. "Stand up Lillie and I will get you home."

Lillie stood and followed the lantern up the mountain and down through the valley. When she tired from the climb, she sat and rested while her father talked with her and assured her safe return. He told her he was not angry, but she must follow him

This is a remnant of the path used by Lillie on the night she was saved by her father's spirit.

exactly or risk a fall. She followed the lantern through the rest of the next mountain and down the valley. She knew they were close to home when she started up the hill by the barn. The fog still covered them like a blanket of mist. Nearing the porch, her father told her to go inside. He had stopped in the yard by the porch, holding the lantern high. Lillie obeyed, thanking God to be home again safe and sound. She turned to thank her father for being there for her, but he was already gone.

The following morning she did not see her father at breakfast. Lillie asked her mother how her father knew she had gotten lost the night before. Her mother looked puzzled for a moment. "We didn't know you were lost last night. I thought you were in bed already from your trip."

It was then Lillie told her story to her mother. Her mother sat in mild shock until Lillie had told all, including hearing her father's voice always ahead of her showing the way home.

Lillie's mother leaned slightly forward and looked her daughter in the eyes. "Lillie, your father was in bed by the time it was dark. He never left the house. It had to be your father's spirit guiding you home."

Lillie never questioned her mother; she just nodded and continued through her day in small wonderment of her father keeping his word to her. When she next saw her father, he never mentioned her being lost or late. He just smiled with a strange little twinkle in his eye.

It was Lillie who said, "When someone truly loves you, never doubt their words."

Selu

Throughout the Cherokee is told a story of a hunter who became desperate to feed his family. Some people believe the story was first introduced by a Philadelphia naturalist named William Bartram, who was exploring the region close to Patton's Run in the Nantahala River Gorge in May 1776. Bartram had spent time with a small band of Cherokee led by Chief Atakullakulla.

It's been reported that the Cherokee told Bartran of a tale where a hunter scoured the mountains for game to feed his family. He had started at sunrise, but did not discover any tracks of any animals. As the sun went down behind the mountains, the hunter sat behind his fire and prayed for his family's needs. He had little to eat himself and soon he lay down to rest. He was exhausted from his search for food. The disappointment in finding nothing left him disheartened.

The hunter dreamed of a beautiful voice singing. The singing continued through the night until the rising sun woke him from his slumber. As he sat upright, the singing seemed to drift away.

The next day, the hunter still could find no sign of any game to feed his family. He searched the valleys and the streams without success. He heard the sounds of neither game nor foul for the entire day.

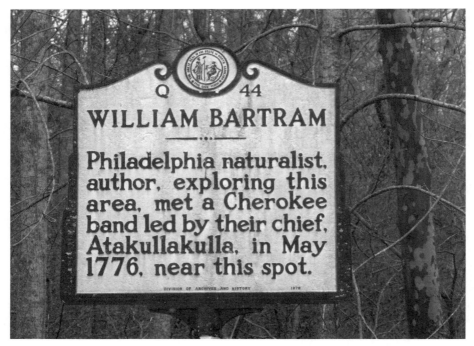

The honoring of the meeting between William Bartram and Chief Atakullakulla can be found here at Patton's Run in the Nantahala National Forest

Evening came and he made a lonely camp once again with nothing to fill his empty stomach but a little water and a few berries from the bushes nearby. As he slept, he had the same dream again, except this time it was so vivid that he believed he was awake and listening. The hunter woke before daylight and was still hearing the beautiful voice singing to him. He knew then his dream had been real and he began to follow the sound of the voice coming to him from the woods.

To the hunter's amazement, the voice was coming from a green stalk of corn. The plant spoke to him and told him to cut roots from the plant and carry them back to his family. They were to be shared with everyone in the village. The plant told him when he returned home the roots were to be chewed the next morning. After he had done this, he was to go get water before anyone else was awake. When this was done, he was to go into the forest, where he would kill many deer for his family and others.

The hunter followed the directions as he was instructed, yet he felt no different than he had before. The hunter had believed there to be magic in the corn stalk's words. Feeling betrayed by a dream, he returned home to gather his bow for another hunt. As the hunter picked up the bow, the beautiful voice returned, this time singing to him. She told him to go back to the water and catch many fish for his family. The hunter did as told, though he doubted what the singing voice was saying to him.

To the hunter's amazement, he caught more and bigger fish than he had ever dreamed. He returned to his family, smiling and happy that he was able to bring such a gift for them.

That night, the hunter dreamed again of the singing voice. She told him to rise before the sun and gather his bow. There would be meat for his family for all time to come. The hunter obeyed. He rose from his bed without waking his wife and gathered his bow. Silently, he left his home, not knowing which way to go. He began to walk west until he reached a small cascade of rapids. Stooping down beside the rapids, he drank deep from the cold clear waters.

The hunter lay down to rest and began to dream. The sweet song filled his head, teaching him all the secrets of the forest and its animals. There was much more to be learned other than a way to kill the animals for food. She taught him to pray and thank the animal for its sacrifice to feed his family. She sang to him many lessons, including that he must never take more than he needs from the forest or the animals and fish. If he heeded his lessons and learned them well, he would never go hungry. All things must remain in balance and respect for life.

The hunter woke from his dream and the sweet voice was no longer to be heard. The form of a woman rose from the ground before him, smiled, and vanished from his sight. From that day forward the hunter became one with all living things and was never hungry again. Most of all, he rejoiced in the things he had learned. When the hunter returned to the village, the elders told him the sweet singing had come to him from Selu, the wife of Kana'Ti, mother of the Cherokee.

The Diligent Nanny

At times, the spirits of people who have passed from this life have lingered on in the places they loved the most. They have attached themselves to the buildings and the belongings they cherished in life. It's not too unusual for families to keep their loved one's treasures just as they had left them as a sort of homage to their memories.

This respect for the deceased is meant to be an honor. The belief in putting aside the items obtained in life by another is a way to assure the dead rest in peace. The question remains, who makes the decision? Is it the living who decides the eternal rest of a loved one or the spirit themselves?

Everyday thousands of young women take their precious children and place them in the hands of those they trust. They are assured their children will be treated with the greatest of care. There are some places that childcare goes far beyond the physical world and their children are protected from beyond. These childcare centers are a wonder to those who work and live with the children.

Within the countryside of Jackson County, North Carolina, a dedicated and loving nanny still cares for and protects the children she once loved so dearly in life. It was her dream to have a daycare center for children. She did everything she needed to do to procure a place where she could fulfill that dream. In a matter of time, a house was found that suited her purposes as closely as possible. Holding her dream like a precious stone, her family and friends helped her do the renovations to the building to accommodate her needs. The fenced in playground held shade trees for the children to play under during the summer months; and room enough on the inside where the children had plenty of space to explore new worlds during the cold winters.

The day came when the children started to gather within her new daycare. She smiled and treated them all as if they were her own. She rocked the babies in her wooden rocking chair and hummed sweetly the lullabies she had learned and sang to her own children. The toddlers knew where to go when they scraped a knee or bumped their head while playing. They all crawled upon Anna's lap knowing she would make everything well.

Anna cared for her children even when the autumn of her life was upon her. Nothing kept her from seeing the children and making sure they were well taken care of. Nothing, not even death, has deterred her from her vigil.

It has been six years since Anna was called away from us. Her daycare center is still open today, filled with children who come to learn and play as they always did. And what about Anna? Well, there was never a time when Anna did not come back to work each day — even after the pastor had spoken his final words and she was placed into the hands of God.

One spring morning, like so many others, the sun shone gently down upon the daycare. Susan drove to the daycare as she did every morning, looking forward to another day. When she arrived, she parked her car in the usual place and mounted the steps to the front door. Her keys jingled lightly as she unlocked the door and

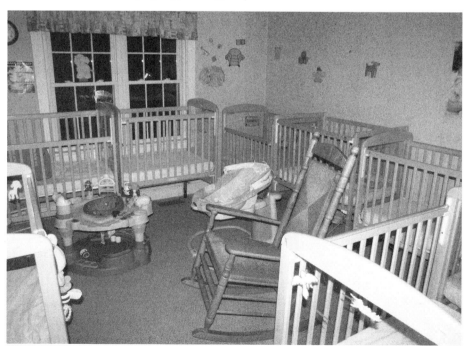

An unseen figure, thought to be that of Anna, appears to rock this rocking chair.

stepped into the toddler's area. The office door lay open before her and she looked at the tiny toy figures Anna had left on the windowsill six years before. Everything in the daycare was still as though Anna would be coming to work at any time. Anna's favorite coffee cup still stays in the kitchen. Her red jacket and slippers are still as she left them in the office, as well as handwritten notes and receipts in her handwriting.

Susan began to turn on the lights as she passed through each room in preparation for the children. As she turned and started up the hallway, a figure walked from the office, crossing the toddler's room, and out through the front door.

Susan could see the figure of a woman quite clearly and there was no mistaking her identity. The woman was none other than Anna. Susan was fully aware of what she had witnessed. The figure was as solid as if Anna was actually there with them. The sight of Anna walking across the room gave her cause to doubt her senses and still it was all too obvious what she had seen!

Susan was not surprised when the haunting continued to happen. She never knew when Anna was going to come to visit the children, but she always made a point to leave her mark on the ladies who worked there.

Sometime later Susan again saw Anna; this time Anna was leaning on a crib in the baby's room. These particular cribs are designed to hold more than one child for evacuation in emergencies. Anna looked at Susan and then slowly faded from sight, leaving Susan breathless.

Susan still kept the cups for the children in the cupboard in the kitchen just as Anna had done while she was in charge of the children's care. With nobody in the kitchen or anywhere close to the cabinet, the cups would suddenly fall from the shelf. No matter how they were placed on the shelf, Susan would find them on the floor. Soon, it was expected for something to be out of the norm and they all knew it could only be Anna.

Children are always entertained when they have marking pens in which to draw a picture. Anna and her employees made sure they were always there for them. It helped to expand the children's minds; drawing was an adventure for their imaginations. The marking pens were kept on a rack next to the sink in the toddler's room — or at least that is where they were expected to be. There are times when these markers gain a life of their own and fall from the rack. Some days it is a regular occurrence. Is this Anna trying to express her wishes? Susan believes it is.

The toys we have in these modern times are certainly different from a child of the 1950s or '60s. Everything these days seems to be battery-operated and there is always an on and off switch. Susan began her usual morning rounds preparing for the day. As she passed the door leading to the room where the cribs are kept, she could see Anna's rocking chair sitting in the middle of the room like the throne of a queen. However, this is not what caught her attention on this particular morning. There was a toy wagon that is kept beneath a crib until it is ready for use by one of the children. It can only be turned on manually, and carries the usual sounds that attract children. Nobody was in the building but Susan, yet the wagon was operating on its own. At the same time, there was an electric infant's swing sitting close to the rocking chair, *swinging* of its own accord. Susan stepped over to the swing and saw, to her dismay, that the switch that made it possible to operate was off!

Susan and another employee began to hear several of the children make a strange request. They said there was a man in the apple tree and wanted him to go away. This would have normally been dismissed as a child's imagination working overtime, but not this time. The children claiming to see the man were not in collusion with each other. The strange man was always seen in the apple tree!

Their age and the manner in which they answered when questioned led the staff to believe them. This man in the apple tree seemed to be a thorn in the side of one child in particular and he described the man without hesitation. The man he described fit the former owner of the house — and there was no possibility the child had ever seen the man before.

Susan yearned to discover what was happening in the daycare center. She contacted a local group of paranormal investigators who immediately accepted her offer to do an investigation. The ghost hunters arrived at the center in the late afternoon. Susan gave them a tour of the center and answered all of their questions. After setting up their equipment, the ghost hunters immediately started photographing everything on the premises in daylight.

There was nothing out of the ordinary in this building. Everything seemed normal, but, soon, the evening sun dipped below the mountains and the center began to change.

The investigators used digital recorders in an attempt to capture any EVPs or voices from beyond the grave. Digital cameras were used for still photographs as well as infrared lighting with the camcorder that they placed in the toddler's room. This was the place where the employees had reported most of the activity taking place.

One investigator, Renee, asked if Anna was there and, if so, to please give them a sign of her presence. Immediately the sound of cabinets being slammed shut in the kitchen reverberated throughout the rooms. The investigators returned to the kitchen — and indeed the cabinets that usually lay cracked open were securely closed!

During the course of the investigation, the ghost hunters were witness to Anna's rocking chair moving on its own volition and cold spots throughout the building. They also captured on tape many different sounds, including a heavy sigh and a female voice calling out "How?" on two occasions!

The investigators had a sensitive with them who discovered the remains of an old garden plot and the presence of a man. The sensitive described what he felt to Susan and she clarified that the man was indeed involved with the history of the property. All of the information provided by the sensitive was correct.

Before midnight, photographs were taken of the exterior of the center. These photographs revealed several bright energy orbs by the apple tree close to the center itself. While the photograph session was producing very good results, one of the investigators caught a bright red light moving inside the window of the infants' room. The light made its way across the room before disappearing. There was no one in the rooms at that time.

The camcorder was capturing some very good results in the toddlers' room as well. Two orbs appeared and rested on the shoulders of Susan and one of her co-workers while the investigators were working with the K-2 meters and other equipment. These meters record electromagnetic energy in the air that is usually associated with paranormal activity — and they started responding to certain questions being asked. In this manner, the group, as well as Susan, was able to communicate with the entity identifying herself as "Anna." The session lasted for almost five minutes before Anna became afraid; she answered one last question before leaving the group. However, Anna did acknowledge that there were children with her and that the man the children described from the apple tree was there also. With the evidence they had acquired, the team reported to Susan that they believed she was in the presence of an intelligent haunt.

The children who come to the center love it here. They feel safe and loved, and I have no doubt that is exactly what happens here daily. Bless you Anna.

The Portal

For as long as theologians have known about Heaven and Hell, followers of the faith have believed there are portals that actually lead to Hell in thousands of places here on Earth. They have reportedly found them in hospitals, homes, wooded areas, mountainous regions, and jungles alike. As to the truth of these locations, little is known other than what those who swear by what they have witnessed. Witnesses have varied from the layman to the professional investigator, and the worshipers of religions that others deem very unorthodox.

Among Native Americans, evil spirits are found in many places also. There are places they deem to be forbidden for their people to visit or go near. There was a time when the Cherokee had found a site to camp and make their spear and arrowheads for hunting. The area was not an outstanding place, yet they later found it to be excellent for watching for intruders trespassing on their lands.

This small plot of land where they made their arrowheads now overlooks the town of Bryson City, North Carolina. Located

To the right of this fireplace is thought to be the portal leading into another realm of existence.

in Swain County, it is a mere ten miles from today's Cherokee reservation.

Every man dreams of owning his own home. During the 1960s, a contractor built a beautiful ranch style house on top of the hill once used by the Cherokee. It possessed all the latest amenities of the era and was very pleasing to the eye. Best of all was the view you had while sitting beneath the shade trees lining the front yard. Whether it was the Fourth of July parade or the Christmas lights of the town below, you could see it all from the privacy of your home.

The family had its usual trials and tribulations in their lives, but they were basically very happy in their new home. Over a period of time, though, things changed — and not for the better! There came a time when the girls would not descend the stairs to the basement unless they had no choice in the matter. When told to summon their brother, they would take a few steps down to the basement only to retreat as quickly as possible. They told of feeling a presence that deeply disturbed them, bordering on fear.

Their brother, who made his bedroom in the basement, had his own problems in the new home. Vivid dreams or nightmares plagued him constantly. He heard disembodied voices and saw full-bodied apparitions. The being who visited him held no restraint in actually touching him or holding him down on his bed.

The entity within the home did not confine itself to just the basement. Two women sat in the cooling shade of the garage on a beautiful spring day. They chatted with each other, laughing and talking the day away. The son and his father sat close by in the living room watching a ball game on the television. Suddenly, the sounds of terrible screams reverberated throughout the house. It made the sound as if the two girls in the garage were being violently attacked! The two men raced for the garage ready to defend their home and their guests, but the girls had not screamed. In fact, everything was very pleasant where they sat. They had not heard anything out of the ordinary. They were enjoying the "peace and quiet" of the mountaintop home. Visibly shaken, the two men returned to watching their game with no explanation for the screams they had heard.

Another occasion brought the men racing to the aid of the matron of the beautiful home. While busy in a room on the other end of the house, they were brought up short by the horrifying screams that sounded like the children's mother. The men raced to where she was sitting and found she had not screamed for help. Not only that, but she had not heard any screaming!

There are people who believe that a demon can mimic the voice of a human being anytime it desires. It is also believed this is done to draw attention to them in an effort to control the inhabitants of a building or area.

These strange and almost frightening events occurred throughout the entire time the family lived in the home. Boys will be boys and every boy invites friends over to spend the night. They talk about everything under the sun until it's time to go to bed and prepare for the next day. The boys gathered in the basement for the sleep-over. Some lay their sleeping bags on the floor in an ante room just off the basement kitchen. At the opposite end of this room is a door leading to a utility room. Not long after midnight one of the visitors was awakened from his sleep. Suddenly, he was assaulted in his sleeping bag by a huge figure that battered and rolled him about the floor in front of witnesses. Standing by the utility door was the sight of what appeared to be the ultimate evil — the figure was so horrific he refused to describe it. The young man grabbed his sleeping bag and clothing, literally running from the house. He never returned.

The years slowly passed and with it comes an age when we all face the reality of infirmity. The father had passed some years earlier, leaving the mother to care for the home. She too became ill. Her bedroom faced the rear of the home looking out over the backyard. Here, she was able to enjoy some of the sights and sounds of nature as she lay resting. Early one afternoon she was laying in bed, reading, with her poodle lying at her feet at the end of the bed. Without warning, the poodle was lifted from the bed by unseen hands and flung violently through the air. The little dog struck the closet door with great force and fell to the floor. Was this the work of a demon in their home? They all began to wonder, especially with the history of the house.

A tall, dark figure would make itself known to the male members of the house; however, *it* would not appear to the ladies. After the mother passed, the family decided to make some updates to the home. They hired a gentleman to come in and do all the repairs they wanted to make. The arrangement was for him to live in the home as he did his work. It was not long before the family found he was locking himself away from the basement at night.

According to the repairman, things were going on that were very disturbing to him. He would hear voices when there was nobody there. Things moved on their own accord, or by unseen hands, and tools disappeared. He never felt like he was alone in the house. At one time, he swore the children were borrowing his tools without his knowledge. This was not the case. Building materials and supplies disappeared as well. There was no logical reason for these things to happen. Before he was able to finish all the repairs, the man had a heart attack and was forced to stay away from the house.

The left side of the basement is a large room. At the very end of it stands a cozy fireplace. For all concerned, you would believe this is a pleasant place to be, yet at times the air is filled with the smell of a burning electrical charge. The smell is very prominent and appears to emanate from the entrance doorway to the room from the kitchen. The sound of the electrical charge could actually be heard with the human ear!

As for the son, his interactions with a being that is other worldly has produced manifestations and dreams that appeared, for all intents and purposes, to be more than just dreams. According to him, the being has been trying to show him something in the house that the others are not aware of. He states there is a portal to the right of the fireplace that leads directly to another world that is very unpleasant. If his beliefs are correct, it is a portal to Hell itself — and he believes he has caught a glimpse of this world.

This bedroom closet is the site where a small dog was lifted from the bed and slammed into the door. The distance was approximately ten feet.

Throughout the sixteenth and seventeenth centuries, the study of demons by theologians determined that demons are both good and bad. According to the teachings of the Catholic Church, all demons are of evil origin. Could this portal be an actual entry into Hell? The fact remains until someone enters one of these portals and returns we will never know. As we live and learn of greater works, we come to find this is another legend whose existence is yet to be proven.

Widow's Walk

Goose Creek Road in Cherokee winds its way through the hills and intersects with Cooper's Creek Road at its end. It lies within the Swain County boundary with Cooper's Creek Road circling back to Highway 19. This road has many campsites for visitors and has stood as a close-knit community for as long as most will remember.

The mountains of North Carolina are no stranger to abstract weather conditions. The winters can be harsh with large snowfalls and freezing temperatures. On the other hand, the summers are very temperate with a soothing cool to keep you comfortable, especially in the higher elevations. Flooding of the creeks and rivers has been a threat since the beginning of time. These rivers and creeks ran long and deep before modern dams and changes in the terrain had taken place. The waters teemed with fish helping the habitants of the area nourish their families.

With the depth of the waters and their rate of flow, it enabled businessmen to build mills to grind corn and wheat into flour for cooking. These mills sprang up in communities throughout the mountains. One very good example of the milling of corn can be seen at Mingus Mill, just beyond the Cherokee reservation on Highway 441. Built in 1886, the mill still operates as though time has never passed them by.

A grist mill much like the one at Mingus is located at the intersection of Goose Creek and Cooper's Creek roads. This mill is now boarded up to keep visitors out and for the safety of the public.

Cooper's Creek by the mill. Close to this spot was where the body of Elias was said to be found. His wife was reportedly seen nearby after she died of old age.

It is also private property. Due to its condition, trespassing on this property could be hazardous to your health. Cooper's Creek ran high and strong for many years. The waters of the creek turned the paddle wheel efficiently and the milling of corn and other products helped the community to prosper. People walked or rode their wagons for miles to bring their products to the mill.

Though local history has not verified any facts, it is rumored the tale of a great flood happened in the area during the 1800s. The waters of Cooper's Creek broached the crest of the sides of the creek and covered the area. The storm, along with the flooding, was said to last for many days. Rock slides and mud covered the paths people used for getting from one place to another. Travel was all but impossible.

A young carpenter named Elias lived close to the creek when the flooding occurred. His wife was heavy with a new child soon to be born to them. Elias's mother had written them and said she was coming to stay until Elias's wife could get back on her feet after the birth of the child. This would have been a great blessing. Elias knew nothing about helping birth the child and was helpless when it came to the care of his wife at this time. He was a man who had worked hard all of his life and knew little of the ways of women or their conditions.

The rain started lightly in the beginning. Elias stared out the window, hoping to see the cart carrying his mother soon. It never arrived. The rain became a deluge of cascading water unlike anything he had ever seen. The heavy wind tore at the shake shingles covering his cabin roof. With the wind howling about the cabin, he watched his wife, knowing her time was near. The dark of night fell upon the little cabin and Elias's wife began to moan softly. She told him the baby was near and he needed to go and find help for her. Elias knew there was someone home at the house by the bend of the creek. He left the cabin and ventured into the night, trying desperately to seek help for his young wife.

During his absence, the rain subsided and eventually stopped altogether. The young mother stood by the window and wondered where her husband could be. Hours had passed with no word of him. A knock resounded through the cabin and the back door flew open with a slam against the wall. From what she had seen, it had opened on its own accord! No one entered or called out to her. She quickly closed the door and hurried back to the window. Coming up the path was a neighbor who lived up the mountain from them. Her husband had cut wood with him and they both went to the same church on Sunday. Walking behind him, with a basket in hand, was his wife.

Elias' wife welcomed them in and asked if they had seen her husband. She explained that the baby was due and he had gone for help during the storm. The neighbor's wife held her close as they told her of someone finding Elias in the bend of the creek. He had fallen and drowned in the roaring flood waters. The young woman collapsed in her arms and they placed her in her bed.

Elias's wife bore a fine young son who grew into a man whom everyone liked. He eventually married and moved away, but never neglected to care for his mother. She died in her sleep at a very old age. Her life slipped away, laying in the same bed she had shared with her husband Elias.

Several years passed by and the old cabin was torn down. Strange sights began to be seen by the creek, including a woman in a plain gingham dress walking by the side of the creek. Before she could be spoken to, she would disappear from sight. Some thought they had imagined the sighting. Others recognized her right away! It was the wife of Elias coming to find her husband. She wore her hair in a tight bun on the top of her head. Her dress was ankle length and of a style long outdated. Her figure was plain to see from a distance, but on closer inspection you could see the creek through her misty form. Her mouth could be seen moving, though no sound was ever heard.

As legends persist in our culture, it is noted that more than one star-crossed lover has come back to search for their loved one. The vows taken at their weddings are very serious and not to be broken...even after death. Has she found Elias? That has yet to be discovered. It is our hope that someday she will find him once again and they will be together for all eternity.

3

Macon County

In 1828, the western part of Haywood County became Macon County. It gained its title in honor of Nathaniel Macon; unknown to most, he not only served in the United States House of Representatives, but also as Speaker of the House from 1801 to 1807. He then went on to serve the rest of his years in the United States Senate.

Through the roaring waters of Nantahala Gorge to the mystical waters of Bridal Veil Falls, the wonders of nature are always at their finest here. White settlers lived together with the Native American tribes, learning from each other. These mountains can be unforgiving to those unaccustomed to the laws of nature. In the light of day or the darkest of night, the essence and spirits of those who walked here before surround you.

Hunter's Moon

A long the Nantahala River, the woodlands are filled with game that entice the hunter. Bear, deer, turkey, as well as small game, run in abundance. There are still many areas of these woods that appear primitive to a degree. The hunt is not easy and can take a hunter far from his home before he realizes what has happened.

This enticing tale originates from Topton, North Carolina, which lies within the boundaries of the great Nantahala Gorge. Its beauty in most respects is unparalleled. During a time when the Cherokee were being hunted for the purpose of relocating them, they hid in the caves along the Nantahala. Its rushing waters disguising any sounds made from everyday life made a long-term stay possible, not to mention providing them with food and shelter.

The Cherokee had taught many Europeans how to hunt within these forests. There were many ways to kill game for their survival. After a number of years, the Europeans favored using dogs for hunting as opposed to still hunting. Unlike the Indians, they never asked for the blessing of the kill. This proved to be a mistake that has killed many hunters and resulted in the loss of their dogs. These hunters saw no reason to honor the Cherokee way and blatantly disregarded the warnings of those who knew the consequences for their deeds. Many a tale has been told of hunters finding themselves lost in the woods at night with no way of getting help.

One of the first examples of this occurred around 1800. There have been no actual recordings of the incident other than the passing of the story from generation to generation. A hunter gathered his hounds and headed for the falls close to what is now River Road. He and his party set up camp by the river and prepared food for the evening. The hunt was in their blood and could barely wait to begin.

As darkness fell upon the hunting party, they sat by the fire sharing stories of other hunts they had participated in over the years. A member of the hunting party, who had hunted the falls

Wolf Run on River Road is designated to be the home of the ghost bear.

before, asked if anyone had ever heard of the Hunter's Moon. The small group of men said they had not, but wanted to hear the story.

"The local people here talk about a Hunter's Moon. During this time they heavily advise against hunting bear up here. According to them, the hounds will pick up the scent of a bear you won't be able to resist tracking. This bear will lead you away from your camp and lose you in the woods...only to appear just far enough ahead of you to make you follow him. You will track him for miles without realizing what you have done before it is too late to turn back."

The bear has changed colors with the passing of the story. Some say he is a big black bear. Others say he has a matted coat with light spots. Another has said he was mixed with a brown bear. All the stories talk about his size and speed.

A hunter sitting close by the fire asked, "You have hunted bear up here for many years, have you seen this bear?"

The hunter stared into the fire and hesitated before answering: "Yes, I have hunted here since I was fifteen with my father. We made the mistake of going on the mountain during the Hunter's Moon. Before the hunt was done, we lost three hounds that were led into the falls by the bear and my father never hunted here again. You understand he saw something up there. He wouldn't talk about it, but he has never hunted anything since that day."

A hunter grinned. "So you believe the bear did that to him and the hounds?"

The man telling the story looked back into the other hunter's eyes for only an instant. "If the locals are right, the bear is not a bear. It is the spirit of a man murdered while hunting that takes his revenge on the Hunter's Moon."

The rest of the hunting party scoffed at the story, not believing in the tales of the mountains. The following day, the party left the camp for the hunt on the Hunter's Moon. All but one left the camp. He said he would hunt for bear the next day, but not

This section of Wolf Run has been cited as being one of the places the scent of the ghost bear is first discovered.

today. The other men left him at the camp and began their hunt for bear. One of the men had bragged his hounds could take any bear that gave up the scent. The storyteller warned him to beware of what he wished for. If the bear appeared to them, it was best to take the dogs off the scent and come back until the bear was gone. They scoffed at the very idea of such an animal even existing.

Darkness fell on the camp with no sign of the other hunters. The sound of the hounds on the scent could be heard clearly across the mountains. He knew they were trailing the Ghost Bear. Every instinct he had told him so. The morning of the third day the hunters returned, some without their dogs. He did not ask them what happened. They were exhausted with scratches and bruises covering their bodies. These were plain to see through the rips in their clothing. One of the hunters returned without his rifle, claiming he lost it in the thicket by the rapids.

The silence of the other hunters was much more than fatigue. It would seem something happened to them to make them believe. The next morning, the men broke camp and returned to the main trail. None of them spoke a word of the hunt days before. The storyteller knew what they had seen and he wished with all his heart he had not agreed to take them to this mountain. No bear hide was worth the price.

Years later, one of the hunters from that night lay on his deathbed. It was here he professed to be face-to-face with the great Bear in the thicket where he lost his rifle. In his fear, he said that the face of the great bear changed with what he swore to be the features of a tortured man. Beware the Hunter's Moon... It could be the last hunt of your life.

The Snow Witch

D eep in mountains of Macon County, near the village of Snowbird, still rings a tale that few will remember. As well as anyone can recall, it was told as late as the early 1800s in this area. It is the tale of the Snow Witch.

As the snow blankets the ground with its beautiful white flakes as soft as angel's wings, it is a time to beware. There was once a woman known for her witchery in the community. When wood would not burn in the fireplace, it was due to the Snow Witch. When children slept ill in their beds and parents worried about their recent sudden misfortune, it was due to the Snow Witch.

The Snow Witch was said to have been a white woman of European descent living among a mix of Cherokee and whites in the community. Where she came from or when is uncertain. Her hair was yellow as gold and her smile as sweet as the cool waters of the Nantahala. Her pale eyes did not smile. She had the look of pure evil with a voice that buried itself deep within your soul. She did not bore fear unless you crossed her. It was then you were sure to be cursed until she saw fit to remove the abomination imposed upon you.

Many scoffed at her reputation. They did not believe in witchery in any form. These people were good, solid Christians and witchery was out of the question! If you had bad luck or dreamt of evil things, it was you who caused it, not a witch! This belief did not support small bits of evidence of her existence or her power to interfere in your life.

There were times when parents would threaten a misbehaving child with a visit from the Snow Witch. This worked very well, as the child usually changed quickly for fear of reprisal from her. One such mischievous child was Jimmy, and he didn't believe anything would be able to hurt him. His parents did everything they could think of to get him settled down like other children his age. All of this was to no avail. Jimmy did what Jimmy wanted, regardless of the consequences.

It was in the winter of 1961 that Jimmy's grandfather came to stay with the family. He had lost his wife to a battle with influenza as many people in the area had at that time. His son asked him to stay with them so he would not be alone. The grandfather was happy to do so. This made it much easier to be with all of his family whenever he desired. He worried about little Jimmy, though. Knowing the direction the little man was headed in life was not a pleasant thought for any parent or grandparent. Society would not tolerate his behavior for long.

Jimmy, in his zeal for excitement, killed one of his grandfather's best hens by playing a game with it. Grandfather was very angry and demanded an explanation as to why he killed the chicken. Jimmy just laughed and said, "It's just an old chicken, who cares!" Grandfather cared enough to spank him for his efforts. After Jimmy's punishment, his grandfather told him the Snow Witch would see to it he did not do anything like that again. His grandfather also warned Jimmy to beware — the Snow Witch would steal his soul if she caught him. Jimmy just laughed and walked away.

That very night after Jimmy had gone to bed the snow began to fall outside his window. It snowed heavily throughout the night covering everything in sight. As Jimmy lay sleeping, he dreamed of making his way to the outhouse through the snow. The snow was deepening at a steady rate. With each step, it was more difficult to traverse. He made it to the outhouse and on his return there came a figure from out of the snow. It was a vile, threatening figure. In his mind, he knew he must make it back to the porch before it could catch him. If he didn't, he feared he would die. The figure steadily gained on him. Just as the figure reached for him, he awoke safe in his own bed. He was sweating profusely from the reality of the dream. He told his mother of the dream he had. She was quick to tell him the Snow Witch was after him for his bad behavior. Jimmy scoffed at this and continued on.

The snow kept Jimmy inside for most of the day. In the evening, it started to snow once more, leaving behind four more inches for the family to deal with. Jimmy slept uneasily this night also. The dream returned with a vengeance. This time Jimmy barely escaped the Snow Witch's clutches. He awoke once again in a cold sweat. Still, he scoffed at the idea of a Snow Witch.

On the third night of the snowstorm, Jimmy was not eager to go to bed. He tried his best to stay awake, but was unable to do so. He was soon asleep, soundly, while more snow fell outside his bedroom window. Once again, he dreamed of making his way to the outhouse through the deepening snowfall. He stepped from the door of the outhouse and made his way toward the back porch of the house.

As in the other dreams, Jimmy saw her from the corner of his eye. She made her way through the snow easily while Jimmy struggled with his each step. Jimmy could almost feel her on top of him. Glancing over his shoulder, he saw the golden hair and pale, almost white eyes of the Snow Witch. She said nothing, but her evil smile said everything. Panic filled his mind and heart as he tried desperately to reach the safety of the porch. He knew if he got there he would be safe. She could not enter the house!

Jimmy leapt onto the porch, grabbing the screen's doorhandle just as the Snow Witch grabbed his collar. He awoke with a start. The dream had been all but too real for him. The rest of the night he lay in his bed not sleeping, but waiting for the rising of the morning sun.

At breakfast, Jimmy sat quietly eating his food. This morning he complained of nothing. He asked for the salt instead of demanding it and, when he had finished eating and cleared his plate, he asked for permission to leave the table. His parents and his grandfather were confused at his new behavior.

Jimmy discovered tiny scratches on the back of his neck by his shirt collar. When he peered out the back door toward the outhouse, there were two sets of footprints in the fresh snow. One set belonged to his little feet. The other, slightly larger, appeared halfway into the backyard, as if they sprang from nowhere, and led to the porch. Yet, none of his family had left the house that morning!

Little Jimmy had turned over a new leaf and grew up to be a fine young man with very well-behaved children of his own. As for the Snow Witch, she still watches, awaiting those who do wrong.

A Lonely Grave

Hidden in the mountains of Macon County is a cemetery close to a deep ravine. The small trickle of water running through the bottom of the ravine can barely be called a creek. In earlier years, the water ran strong with the purest of life's treasure.

The cemetery was placed here by the cool waters for those who made the long journey to tend to the graves of their loved ones. The graves date back to before the Civil War. It is no longer kept and tended by loved ones. It is overgrown with the vegetation of the area and the graves are barely visible. It is almost forgotten by everyone except a few who visit here often.

However, those who do visit have not come to tend the homes of the dead. No, they have come to see the spirit of Hannah. The markings on her tombstone have become very indistinct through the years. You would have to know exactly where she is buried to be capable of finding her. There is one other way, though, to locate her grave: If you are fortunate enough to be close by when she appears, she will guide you to her resting place.

This is no ordinary cemetery. The graves here mark the bodies of men who made their share of mistakes in life and it was not for the better of mankind. Some were defending family and honor. Others did their deeds out of revenge for an injustice done to them. In years past, when this cemetery first gained its notoriety for being haunted, people came to see the ghost of Hannah. They soon found there was much more to this plot of land than the spirit of a young woman appearing to them. It was rumored there was something here incredibly evil.

There was the tale of two young men renowned for their bravery in the community. They were rough and more than willing to fight at the slightest provocation. With their reputations, you knew they were not to be bothered. The two young men decided they would brave the tales of the cemetery and find the truth out for themselves. They ventured into the cemetery late at night with flashlights in hand seeking the truth.

The men encountered much more than they bargained for! They returned that evening and quietly slipped into their homes. The following day, and all the rest of the days of their lives, they were changed men. The encounter had left them as meek as lambs. Neither man would tell what had happened to them. Just questions about them being there brought fear to their faces. Soon, the day came when old age brought them to their own deathbeds. They still would not tell what they had witnessed on that night close to the grave of Hannah. Were they able to see Hannah? No. Instead, they witnessed something far more frightening...something from beyond the grave that changed their lives forever.

As for Hannah, she was a blossom in the sun when she walked these mountains. It was said she was as sweet as honey and as pretty as a rose in bloom. What happened to bring her here? There have been many stories regarding her demise. Reportedly, she was to be married to a young man from a nearby community. It was to be a wedding everyone would remember. The couple was not well known nor were they wealthy. It was just a communion between two people who seemed blessed by the angels themselves. They married standing on the mountainside by the Laurel. A few short years later Hannah's husband died in his sleep. The cause of his death was never discovered. Hannah was devastated! Nothing anyone could do gave her peace. She died of a broken heart, her grief too much to bear.

Over the years since Hannah left us, she has been seen dozens of times standing or walking through the small cemetery on the hill. A young man and his wife were amateur ghost hunters and had heard the tale of Hannah. They wanted to witness her appearance for themselves. They visited the site over three summers while vacationing in the mountains and, just as they were beginning to believe it was all a hoax told by some of the local people, they claim to have actually witnessed Hannah making herself known to them!

The young couple left early in the day hoping to get some good photographs of the local color before beginning their final hunt of the cemetery and the mountainside. As evening began to fall, they rested beneath an old silver maple tree. When you come to a place that is noted for having an apparition, the chances of witnessing the phenomena is always small, but for them it was better than no chance at all. They literally prayed for a chance to capture the spirit on film for others to see.

The hours crawled by slowly and a damp chill filled the air. It was disconcerting to feel this chill knowing the temperature to still be hovering in the 70s. The young woman looked off to her right in the direction of where they believed Hannah to be at eternal rest. Her husband gasped slightly and grabbed her arm — ten feet from the spot where they supposed Hannah lay, a heavy mist had formed and was moving slowly to their left. Its form became more distinct with every step it took and within minutes they witnessed what appeared to be a young woman with her head in her hands, sobbing. The small sounds of her crying echoed through the cemetery. Without warning, the sobbing suddenly ceased and the ghostly figure turned toward them ever so slightly, disappearing before their eyes.

The sighting lasted for several minutes. Seeing Hannah had upset the two young people in such a way that they were spellbound and they suddenly realized they had not taken a single photograph!

In their zeal to find out more information about Hannah, and possibly the reason she was crying, they delved deeper into the story. Though they could not verify the "facts," some of the older people in the valley said Hannah would make herself known to people because she was looking for someone to help her. Hannah had lost the love of her life, but, when she died, her family buried her in a place far from her husband. They could not be at rest together. It would seem there was a disagreement between the families as to where the young couple should spend eternity. Hannah was a Baptist, her husband and his family were Methodist.

It was said by several of the good people of this mountain that Hannah needs to be with her husband. The local preacher's thoughts echoed the words from the wedding ceremony: "What God has joined together…."

A Witch for Water

Water is not always easy to find when you are digging a well for your home. In the mountains near the Highlands, before men had machines to dig for them, deep wells were dug by hand. These provided cool clean drinking water for families as well as a cooling place to keep milk from their cows fresh. Root cellars were used for vegetables and the storage of fruit for the family. An average household had a chicken coop for keeping their chickens. Fresh eggs were a must and there was little money to buy them from others. Their homes were as self-sustaining as possible. Usually a household only purchased necessities from a dry goods store. These items were usually salt, sugar, and material for making clothing. Their flour would be ground at a local mill from the harvest of their own crops. A barter system was widely known for many things, including the valuable meat products such as hogs, cattle, and hunting dogs. From an early age, you learned to shoot and kill game with one shot. The price of ammunition was expensive. The price for using more than one shot was wasteful.

Benjamin came to the Highland mountains at an age when he worried for nothing. Youth was on his side and he was a robust young man who feared nothing. He had saved his money and made his way to America from England. He had tasted war and all that comes with it. Benjamin wanted to be as far from war as he could travel and he chose this mountain. Few were willing to sell him

Supposed site of Benjamin's homestead... Is this where he made his bargain with a witch?

any land for a new home. A new home close to a creek could not be found regardless of what you offered to pay. He was not a rich man and settled for a small plot of land bordering a small valley. It held everything he desired except for life-giving water.

Within months, he had cleared the land and was building a new cabin. The timber on the property was used for the log walls of the new home. Though modestly built, he felt it was enough room for a small family to live for a very long time.

Benjamin knew of a small creek a mile from his property and would make the trek daily with his buckets to bring water back to the new house. The neighbors would sometimes help him carry water and store it in barrels for future use. He also caught water in rain barrels for bathing. It was good for a while, but he still needed a well. He attempted to dig three, four wells on the property without success. Witching for water is a time old tradition using dowsing rods. If you have water on your property, the dowsing rods will find it for you. Benjamin hired a man from Cullowhee who was well-known for his dowsing abilities. If there was water to be found, he would find it. His efforts found there to be no trace of water on the property. The man from Cullowhee charged him nothing for his services and left him wondering what he was to do. He could not go on making the trek for water every day.

A week later Benjamin was sitting on the front porch of his cabin, wondering what he was going to do. The man he purchased the land from quickly told him that he never guaranteed there was water on the property and he would not buy it back from him. As he sat smoking his pipe, he became very angry, his dream seeming all but lost. Suddenly, an old woman appeared at his gate. He did not know her, but invited her to sit and talk with him.

She was very old in appearance and dirty. Her voice crackled with age as she spoke to him. "I am told you need water for your cabin."

Benjamin smiled faintly. "Yes, a man from Cullowhee says there is none on the property."

The old woman's eyes narrowed as she spoke to Benjamin. "He knows nothing. Will you strike a bargain with me if I give you water?"

Benjamin laughed at the old woman. "I would. If you were the Devil himself, I'd bargain with you."

The old woman grinned slyly. "Tis' true I'm not the Devil, but for the price of your third child you will have everything a man can ask for."

Benjamin laughed mightily. "You have my word, old woman, and may the Devil take us both if I lie."

The old woman rose from her chair and touched his forehead. The touch felt like a branding iron on his skin. When Benjamin looked up, she was already crossing the gate. Later the following day, the old woman came to his gate again. Benjamin talked with her leaning on her every word. "Within a fortnight you will have your water as well as a pretty young bride. You will have all I have promised and more." The last of her words felt more of a warning than a blessing.

Benjamin did not see the old woman again for many years after that day. He married a lovely young woman of sweet temperament and she gave him a son. His crops were never equaled and he prospered with every dawning of a new day. It was true he had everything a man could ask for. On the eve of his son's third birthday, the old woman was seen standing in his cornfield. He left his barn and walked toward her. She raised her hand for him to stop. In her ancient voice, she declared he was soon to be the father of a baby girl. She turned and disappeared back among the cornstalks.

Benjamin walked back to his cabin and told his wife what the old woman had told him. His wife said it was true. She had found out that very morning she would have another child. Benjamin rejoiced with the news and yet in the back of his mind the words of the old woman rang clear: "For the price of your third child."

All was soon forgotten shortly after the birth of his daughter. He now had many friends he came to rely on for things he needed. His reputation in the community was unrivaled. He had never told his wife of the bargain he had struck with the old woman. He didn't think he ever would for the sake of his marriage.

Late one summer evening Benjamin walked to his well to draw water for his wife's bath. Looking over the side of the well, he saw the reflection of the old woman. To his surprise, her voice crackled through the evening air. "In one year, you shall have your third child and I will have my due." The face then dissolved before him in the tiny ripples of water. Benjamin slammed the bucket into the water and drew deeply from the water. He decided he would be damned before he would give the old woman any of his children. He did not believe that she had been able to give him the things he had worked so hard for through the years.

The prophecy came true to Benjamin on the third day of September the following year. His wife held in her arms another son. Benjamin beamed with pride. For two years he never saw the old woman or heard her voice. Satisfied she would not be there to take his child, he continued his life as a Christian man.

On the child's third birthday, Benjamin came in from the fields to eat his dinner. The stove was cold and his wife had dressed the child for travel. He asked her where she was going. His wife told him it was time for them to go. The other children would be staying, but the youngest would be leaving with her. Benjamin protested and demanded she stay, but, if she had to go, at least leave the child. His wife walked to the door and out before he could protest further. Running for the door he reached the porch, but his wife was already crossing the gate. She turned to face him and, to his amazement, it was the face of the old woman staring back at him. "I gave you what we bargained for and now I have taken my due." With this said, she and the child vanished from his sight.

Benjamin had made a bad deal with a witch. It was within a few short years everything the witch had given him was slowly taken away, including the children. When he had lost everything, he went to the well to draw water only to find it was bone dry. On his deathbed, he told the story of the bargain with the witch to his closest friend. Benjamin told his friend the witch had lived up to her bargain, but the price was too high. His last words was a prayer of forgiveness.

The land yielded little more than a few scrawny trees from that day forward. It is one small plot within a national forest that some say will never be of use for anything.

The Roan Mare

I n the early 1700s, Macon County was still a land of great discovery. Small farms were being built along the mountainsides and valleys for immigrants to raise their families. It was a land of abundance, and life was peaceful for the most part. The Native Americans of the area treated the settlers kindly and tried to interact with them with the gift of sharing. For many, this was more than enough, knowing they could count on their fellow man to help them if they were in need.

With time also came the greed of their fellow man for ownership of lands that were not for sale at any price. The disagreements between the Native Americans and the settlers grew until the two nations were at war with each other. Both sides were unable to come to an agreement. All treaties were broken by the settlers in their bid for taking the land they wanted for themselves.

The Native Americans believed the land was not for sale because it was the property of the Great Spirit and not man. They had boundaries for their lands, but not ownership. The settlers turned a deaf ear and demanded the land at any price. Bloodshed ensued and the happiness they all once knew was no more.

There were many men who refused to fight the Cherokee and Catawba. They kept on a peaceful and friendly basis with all the tribes they encountered. These men did not possess the greed of some of the other factions entering the territory.

Duncan Fein was a man of peace. He wanted no part of any war or words of anger directed toward others. He believed in each man's right to live his own life. Duncan was the husband of Mave, an Irish lass with bright red hair and a temperament to match. They say opposites attract. This being the case, Duncan and Mave were a match made in heaven. They immigrated to the United States from Ireland during a time when Ireland was at war with England in more ways than one. Duncan came to North Carolina with his wife and son looking for a peaceful place for them to live.

In the early 1700s, Duncan settled down in a small cabin some few miles from Bridal Veil Falls on US 64. He used the money he

The river gorge is three miles from Duncan's farm... This is where his body was reported to be found.

had saved to purchase a small plot of land close to the gorge. Here, he cleared the land with a borrowed team of oxen from a nearby farm and paid them in return from his first crop. His honesty was not to be questioned.

With the growth of his family, Duncan added two more rooms onto his cabin. It was a fine home for them and he had made all of the furniture by hand. Duncan was a man of many talents. He knew that to survive and have things for his family he must utilize his skills.

Word came one afternoon that traders were coming to a small town nearby looking for people who wanted to sell furs and hides. Duncan walked to town and struck a bargain with the men.

For the next five years Duncan traded and sold furs and hides with the men from the east at a handsome profit. Duncan and Mave did not become rich, but they were very comfortable knowing they could purchase anything they needed without credit. His crops were good and he also built carriages and furniture for those who wanted it. Time was one thing Duncan had little of.

Winters were always very tough on families during this time. The heavy snows and sickness often came when least expected. During a particularly brutal winter, a stranger made his way through the snow and rapped upon Duncan's door. The stranger was invited to stay until the snow abated and he would be able to continue his journey. Duncan and Mave were surprised he had come into the gorge just to see Duncan.

The stranger brought with him news of what the settlers were planning to do with the Native Americans. They had sent for militia men to capture them and they were to be held in a newly built stockade. He said it would end their ways once and for all. Duncan asked what all of this had to do with him. The stranger said he was sent to get Duncan to talk with the Native Americans and convince them to surrender. Duncan would be made an officer in the militia with full pay if he would do this.

This was an insult to Duncan. He was not a man who would betray his friends for any price. The stranger became menacing and threatened Duncan. He told him that if he did not do this he would be branded a traitor and punished for his crime. Duncan stood to his feet and denounced the stranger for threatening him in his own home. He demanded he leave immediately and the snow be damned!

The stranger stood on the porch of the cabin and gave his parting words: "Beware Duncan Fein, this is not the end of this." Duncan slammed the door and went back to his fire. Within a few short weeks, the snow cleared and Duncan met with two Cherokee he had befriended. He told them of the stranger's words and warned them to go back and tell their people. The Cherokee already knew of this man and had hunted him through the snow. He escaped them through the waters of the Nantahala.

The signs of spring soon fell upon the face of the land. Duncan went into town to sell his furs. One of the buyers had a fine roan mare that caught Duncan's eye. The two men bargained for the mare and Duncan became the new owner of the finest horse in the mountains. The mare was smart and agile, so riding her was a pleasure. Duncan would let nobody near her for fear of the horse being stolen from him. It was his prized possession.

Duncan built a fine carriage for his family to ride to church. The mare was never allowed to pull the carriage; she was always tied to the back. Word came to him that the fighting had worsened between the settlers and the Native Americans. Duncan had seen the warriors cross his land, but they never talked to him anymore. A short trip into town for supplies brought back a bad memory for Duncan. As he stepped lightly from the porch of the general store and mounted his horse, a voice from behind spoke sharply to him. "My, my, that is a mighty fine horse you have Mr. Fein."

Duncan whirled in his tracks — the stranger who had threatened him before was standing in the shade by the corner of the store. Before Duncan could speak, the stranger continued: "That horse is much too fine for a traitor like you. I told you it wasn't over, Duncan, you should have listened."

The stranger turned and walked away as Duncan cursed him for the cur that he was. Duncan rode away, back through the mountain pass headed for home. Darkness came and Duncan had not returned from his trip. Mave worried for him. He had never been late before and she feared something had happened to him. Her fears were confirmed when the mare came into the yard without Duncan. She was winded and lathered as though she had run for her life.

Mave grabbed the reins and took the mare to the barn. She then sent her eldest son to the nearest neighbor for help. However, it was too dark to go looking for Duncan... They would have to wait until morning.

The rising of the morning sun brought half of the community out to the Fein cabin. They began their search and found Duncan shortly after noon. He lay face down near the creek with a single bullet in his back. The only hoof prints were those of the roan mare he prized so highly. Duncan had not been robbed of his money or the other possessions he had on him, and his pistol was still tucked into his belt.

Members of the community immediately thought he had been shot by Native Americans in the area. When questioned, though,

Bridal Veil Falls gains its name from the illusion one sees when the cascading waters run from a forty-foot high waterfall. It is located three miles from the rocks where Duncan Fein was shot. Duncan's mare has reportedly been seen and heard over many years by witnesses of true faith and sound mind.

they were able to show they were not close by when Duncan was murdered. This left only the stranger to question and he could not be found. Yet, regardless of proof, some of the neighbors still blamed the Indians. A month after Duncan was laid to rest someone came to the Fein farm and shot the prized mare. They set fire to the cabin, but it was discovered in time to save the dwelling from being destroyed.

Mave never felt safe on the farm again. She sold the property, and she and her family were said to have moved to Tennessee to try and avoid the ongoing war. As time flows like the waters of life, memories sometimes become real to others. Neighbors of Duncan Fein told of seeing the roan mare running through the gorge headed for the old homestead. They could see her plainly with the stirrups of Duncan's saddle bouncing each time her hooves hit the dirt beneath her — only to disappear when she neared the road. Others claim to have heard a rifle shot before seeing the mare. These people never knew the story of Duncan Fein.

The new owners of the Fein cabin told many about hearing the sound of a horse breathing heavily close to the porch on several evenings. The smell of animal sweat also permeated the air.

It is now 2012 and the world is a far different place than it was in 1700. We are educated and civilized to the point that we want proof of anything we can't explain. The roan mare has not been seen in many years that we are aware of. There have been no reports and the area is visited by thousands of tourists and hunters each year. Will the roan mare ever be seen or heard again? There are some of us who would truly like to see her with her mane flowing in the wind.

4

Cherokee County

C herokee County was formed in 1839 and named in honor for the Cherokee Indians who inhabited the area before their forced removal in 1838. The Cherokee suffered broken promises from President Andrew Jackson after he had sworn himself as their ally. The tribe helped him win the wars against other Indian nations believing he wanted to live in peace, but the Cherokee, as well as others, knew nothing of the Indian Removal Act that Jackson had approved in 1830.

In 1835, the New Echota Removal Treaty was signed and placed into effect — and 17,000 Indians were removed from six states. After enduring bitter cold weather, one of every six Indians died on this march. Cherokee County was one of the points of the beginning of "The Trail of Tears." Andrew Jackson and the men who stood with him were never forgiven for their treachery...the ghosts of the Cherokee and Catawba still echo their names through these hills.

Lessons to be Learned

L ife in the hills of Cherokee County is much the same as anywhere in the North Carolina Mountains. Their heritage comes from the many cultures that settled here from other countries as well as the descendants of the Native Americans. Clinging to the ways of the generations before them, there are still those who believe in the old superstitions. Donald grew up in a family who strongly believed in the old ways and still practices those beliefs.

Donald lost his mother at an early age and feels he learned from the experience. He attributes his beliefs and practices of everyday life to the teachings of his father and all those close to him while he was young. He is a Christian and feels the ways of the Lord are mysterious indeed. This is the story of his lessons learned when his mother passed away.

"Summer of 1940 was more than just another summer. It was a change for my family and friends we would not forget. It was a time of great loss and sadness. We lived a life of hard labor and lean times near the Nantahala River.

"Mother was very ill. The entire family knew she had little time left on this Earth and stayed close to her tending to every need. The doctor sent her home to be as comfortable as she could be in her last days with the words no one wanted to ever hear: 'We have done all we can… It's in the Lord's hands now.'"

There was more to this than just her comfort. The price of a hospital bed was out of reason for a family of their means. Not to mention the fact they would rather have that bed for someone else whose body would mend and could pay for their services.

Their home was modest, but clean and neatly furnished. Father had always had food of some kind on the table to feed his many children. They never had the best and yet they did not go without the things they really needed.

"When mother became ill and could no longer do ordinary tasks, everyone was there to help as best they could, children as well as neighbors. There was not a single family in the area considered well-to-do, but they were always there for each other sharing the little they had.

"In the heat of the summer, the windows were left open to try and create as much circulation of air as possible. The little room in which she lay barely held her bed and two small cane back chairs. This was the room that had the best breeze wafting its way through the shingle house. Not all the windows had screens to keep out flies and any other insects a life in the country had to offer its inhabitants.

"I sat in the hallway watching and listening to mother's labored breathing and wishing times were different. The old folks said it was a waste of time, but I still dreamed of better days. My aunt had gone into the kitchen to fix supper for father, knowing he would be plenty hungry after being in the fields all day. I almost rolled out of my chair when I heard father's heavy boots bound up on the porch like a man possessed. I can still hear his voice as he yelled from the porch, 'Close Ginny's window! Be quick, boy, or she'll be gone for sure.'

"Without a second thought, I jumped from my chair and slammed mother's window shut. We never questioned what we were told to do. You were raised to do it first and then they would tell you the reason for your actions. You were never told but once unless you enjoyed cutting your own switch for them to beat you.

"Father made his way into the house through the back door and headed through the house until he reached the front screen door. I saw him with the broom in his hand trying to keep a white dove from breaking through the screen. The dove attacked the screen several times and was refusing to give up his attacks until father finally slammed the front door closed and locked it.

"I went back to mother's room and watched intently. The dove left the front door and went around the house to mother's window. You could hear its wings fluttering against the glass of the window. The dove tried to get into the house twice more before the sun set behind the mountain.

"I saw the fear in my aunt's and father's eyes. As a child, I had no idea why the dove was trying so hard to gain entry into the house. After supper, my father and I sat on the front porch talking. I asked him why the dove was trying so hard to get into the house and why it scared him so. This is where I learned of some of the ways of the Lord.

"Father drew deep on his pipe and began to speak in a low clear voice. 'There are lessons in this world you need to learn and never forget. What you saw today and other things I have already taught you are good things to know. One day you'll have young'uns of your own and you need to know the things I been tellin' you. A white dove tryin' to get in your house is the sign of a death. That dove today was tryin' to get to your mother. Most say he's God's messenger, kinda like an angel, but you don't know for sure. He come for your mother's soul that's for certain. Tonight I'll pray about it and decide from there whether to let him in or not. I just wasn't ready today to lose your mother.'

"I thought about this for a long time. A white dove is a wondrous sight. I had never seen a dove that looked like that one. Two days later the dove returned to mother's window. It made its way into the room, circled mother's bed, and flew back out. I went to the window and could not see any sign of the white Dove. I wondered how it could disappear so quickly. When I turned from the window, my aunt had a small tear running down her cheek, 'I'm sorry, but Ginny is gone.' Mother passed from us the minute the dove circled her bed.

"Within a day or two after burying mother in the north end of the pasture, we found a wild white rose growing on the grave already in bloom. Father smiled and told me that it was a sign that mother was in the arms of the Lord."

Moon Eyes

Barely across the Georgia state line stands a large stone marker for a dubious journey made to these lands by Prince Madoc. A Welsh nobleman, Madoc was weary of the civil war in his country and set sail with his brother in 1170, landing close in to what is now Mobile Bay, Alabama. According to legend, he and a few followers scouted the countryside, finding everything to their satisfaction.

Madoc was ready to move in. He then left a few of his followers behind and returned to his homeland with the intent of recruiting others to join him on the new land. He successfully recruited enough people and gathered enough supplies to fill ten ships. They set sail for the land they had found and were never heard from again.

Fort Mountain is a state park just beyond the North Carolina/Georgia border. It is believed the stone fort was built before the time of Columbus coming to the Americas. According to legend, the Moon Eyed people, after warring with the Creek and Cherokee nations, lost the battle and moved further north and west into Hiawassee, close to Murphy, North Carolina, before being forced into Tennessee. The war between the Moon Eyed people and the Cherokee is just another version of the same tale.

It is not clear when the Moon Eyed people became nocturnal, and today it's still very much a mystery. Yet they were spoken of as being nocturnal with their homes built below the surface. They were described as being extremely short in stature with pale white skin and beards. The Moon Eyed people seemed very human in all their characteristics and form. Their eyes were large and the slightest glimmer of light made it very difficult for them to see. This was due in part to a subterranean life.

The Moon Eyed people were driven from their homes by the Creek Indians under a full moon, making sight very difficult for them to successfully flee their attackers. When they fled north, the Moon Eyed people took up their nocturnal habits once again deep in the mountains of North Carolina, close to the Tennessee border. The Cherokee believe they were a memory of European settlers before Columbus, making the legend seem to match with the Welsh legend of Prince Madoc.

The story of the Moon Eyed people became widespread and piqued the interest of the great explorers Lewis and Clark.

There is no evidence of Lewis and Clark ever "looking for Welsh Indians" during their explorations. Another interesting note for history: Gwynedd, the Welsh king, never had a son named Madoc and Madoc's journey was a great piece of propaganda produced by the King near 1580 to enrich England's claim to the Americas against Spain, which, much to the chagrin of the English monarchy, controlled colonization of the New World during this period.

The stone wall attested to have been used for the battle of the Moon Eyed people and the Creek Indians stands today in Fort Mountain State Park. It is 850 feet in length and stands six feet tall at its highest point along the ridge. What is the truth behind this battle? Who were the Moon Eyed people? The search continues for the truth.

5

Caldwell County

Caldwell is a small county bordered by the Blue Ridge Mountains and Brushy Mountain. It is a county rich in heritage for those who live there. The climate is mild with elevation changes that run from 900 to 5,964 feet. It is the sharpest change in elevation in the state of North Carolina. The older generations are more in tune with the stories and beliefs of their ancestors.

From the Native Americans come tales to enchant the young and old from other lands. These stories are told year after year at festivals and in books written about Caldwell County. Some of the tales were already being handed down before the first White settlers came to live here in the 1700s. The earliest recorded description of Caldwell County was made by Bishop Spangenberg in 1752. Grider's Fort, built to protect the settlers, was built in 1776. Today, the site of the fort is where the former Lenoir High School was located.

The House Love Built

There are luxurious manors throughout the state of North Carolina. Biltmore House is impressive indeed, but one stands immortal in its indefinable beauty. It was built as a revivalist colonial home in the 1800s for Moses and Bertha Cone. The Cones were industrialist originating from the great state of Maryland. He originally built the impressive manor as a summer retreat for his wife and their guests.

Moses spared no expense with his retreat. The grounds are beautifully landscaped and he actually had white-tailed deer imported from another state to roam the extensive grounds. The home was furnished in excellent taste, with each room accentuated with the grace of true elegance. Located just outside Blowing Rock in Caldwell County, the Biltmore House was — and still is — a masterpiece of architecture.

Moses was unable to revel in its beauty for long. He passed from us at a young age and his wife, Bertha, continued his legacy for another thirty-nine years until she succumbed to the frailties of old age. In the years following, the estate was donated to the National Park Service for the enjoyment of all who care to visit.

Over the years park rangers and guests have reported strange occurrences in the manor. It is not only the sound of but the actual opening and closing of doors without the assistance of the hand. Some have claimed the existence of what they believe to be the spirit of a woman that was once the sister of Bertha Cone. Bertha and Moses are buried on a hillside close to the manor — and legend has spoken of the gravesite being haunted by their spirits.

It has been made apparent to the park service employees that Bertha and Moses will not be separated. The paintings of Bertha and Moses Cone have also taken on a life of their own. They were placed in one of the main rooms directly across from each other. While an effort to redecorate the manor by the park service was not in disrespect to the former residents, their actions did not suit the spirits of the house. The park service placed

The house that love built. The summer home of Bertha and Moses Cone.

both paintings side-by-side on the same wall. This made the spirits unhappy and the following morning both paintings were discovered on the floor, leaning against the wall, one against the other. The portraits were returned to their original places and all returned to normal.

When Bertha Cone passed in 1947, all of the furniture in the manor was dispersed among family members. On a floor where all of the furniture had been removed and completely void of anything, guests have reported hearing the sounds of moving furniture above them. Rangers inspected the area only to find they were the only ones on that floor with nothing in sight. Bertha was known to demand that the back door leading to the kitchen stay closed at all times. Artisans bringing in their wares left the door propped open for convenience until they could finish moving the heavy objects — and then watched as the heavy door closed on its own before their eyes!

The master bedroom once belonging to Bertha and Moses is also no stranger to ghostly activity. A guest sleeping there closed the door on no less than three occasions during the night. On the third awakening, he placed a chair from the room beneath the handle to secure the door. The next morning, he found the chair back in its earlier position against the wall with the door wide open.

The sound of soft piano music has been heard throughout the manor in the late hours of the night. One of the rangers who was staying close by answered the call when an alarm was sounding. He entered the manor expecting an intruder. In the beginning, he could find nothing out of place. Turning to leave, he saw a young girl standing by the stairs. He gave chase as she flew up the stairs. He was unable to catch her before she entered a room at the top of the stairs. The ranger could not open the door without great effort. When he was finally able to enter the room, it was empty — not a living soul could be seen.

Reportedly, Bertha had requested that the home not be used after her passing, but her wish was not to be. The sounds of footsteps in the upstairs hall are not out of the norm, according to some who have been in the house for many years. The gift shop located downstairs is visited regularly by someone who cannot be seen. By the cash register, with nobody close by, corks rose from the shelf and flew across the room, striking the opposite wall. In the office adjoining the foyer was a counter used for keeping a record of the number of guests who visited the manor. Without warning, it began to click as if someone was using it. When the ranger came in to open the office, she was asked to check the apparatus; the count from the day prior should have been "0," but, instead, she was looking at 180. When the ranger and the hostess returned from the kitchen, the count had increased to 286. There was no reason for this. The witness stated the only way the apparatus stopped its behavior was when the hostess called out, "Please stop...you are scaring me!" It worked!

Pictures that are hung carefully on the walls are found on the floor behind the shelving unharmed. Police officers have been called during the night to check the manor for intruders. The sounds and sights were enough to make them call for backup — only to find the building totally void of anything living.

The entity in the manor has no sympathy for male visitors who have come to spend the night. They are the ones who usually have the most problem with the house. A student reported she was upstairs when she became frightened. She ran down the stairs and it was discovered she had three heavy red marks across her back. She never returned to the house. The carriage house is used for restrooms today. It has been said that while cleaning the restrooms at any time you never have the feeling you are alone.

These tales have no verifiable proof other than the word of the witness. The witnesses seem to be of sound mind and body and not prone to exaggerate. Clairvoyants and psychics have stated what they feel here privately to the employees. Professional photographers have seen many unexplained anomalies appear in their photographs of the manor house. Orbs of light on the stairs by the foyer and throughout the house...these anomalies have appeared for years. Everyone who has experienced something here on a regular basis is quick to tell you the house gives you the impression you are always safe here. It is a comforting feeling the minute you step foot into the open foyer.

A very sad story evolved from the years concerning the resting place of Moses Cone. It was said grave robbers removed him from his resting place after hearing he may have been buried with valuable jewels. There were no jewels, but some have said his body was left leaning by his grave.

Legends are like good works of fiction. Where you find fiction, there is often a spark of truth in an effort to make the story more believable. Bertha and Moses Cone built a vision of beauty. The love they had for each other reflects every corner of this property. If their spirits have indeed decided to stay within these walls, it is only so they can be in a place that they loved and where they were happy together.

The manor is open to the public and, whether you are a believer in their presence or a skeptic, this is a home you may find the essence of two people who left their spirits to welcome those who enter their home. The stories above are a few of what guests have claimed to have encountered.

Blowing Rock

C aldwell and Watauga counties both have the distinction of being associated with the town of Blowing Rock. This little town is known as the "Crown of the Blue Ridge." It has seen the sorrows of the Civil War. The town was a source of refuge for families during the war and their husbands and fathers eventually came back here to settle after the war ended.

Before the Civil War, this area saw the wars of Americans against the tyranny of British rule. Taxation without representation was the cry of the day and with this came the call to arms from all citizens. The end of the war left a new nation and the beginning of a new era.

American Indians have never been a stranger to war, whether it is the war in Afghanistan today or war between the tribes in times long before the first European ever saw the coast line of North America. The Cherokee and the Catawba were at war with each other reportedly for as long as a century. This would depend on who you would want to believe. The accounts of the war between them vary greatly and make it difficult to understand as to when the war first started.

A legend has circulated throughout this area for as long as anyone can remember. People today say the legend is a work of fiction. Others are not so sure. They have all visited the rock where it is said to have all begun. The story of Romeo and Juliet and the family feud between the Hatfields and McCoys both have several things in common: young love. The love was forbidden by members of both families and ended in tragedy for all.

Young hearts cannot always understand the reasons why two cultures are fighting to the death. Throughout history two people from opposing sides have eventually met and fallen in love. It is a human emotion that we have no control over, and the Catawba and the Cherokee were no exception to the frailties of the human heart.

By the John's River Gorge is a large rock known as Blowing Rock. It gathered its name from the wind currents that travel through the gorge. Here is where the legend begins.

This way to Blowing Rock! This is a breathtaking view for those who love an age old mystery.

A young warrior reached his manhood in a time when war was raging between the Catawba and the Cherokee nations. He knew his duty to his clan and defended them on many occasions when the terrors of battle lay before him. He was brave and had earned his reputation for being a fierce warrior.

It was a day when he, along with others of his tribe, came to the mountaintop to spy on their enemies. He saw no warriors, but he did see an Indian maiden of such beauty that his life would be changed forever. From first sight he had given his heart to her. He told no one of the maiden and returned to the mountain every time he was able hoping to see her.

He lay trying to sleep at night with little success. Each time he closed his eyes, her face was all he could see. He heard the laughter and saw her smile. His heart ached for her, knowing a life with her could never be. He thought once of kidnapping her and bringing her back to his village. The young warrior banished this idea quickly for fear someone may want to harm her and she would despise him for his actions.

The warrior did not know she had also seen him on one of his trips to the mountaintop. She wished she could speak with him. To not know his name was painful for her to endure. He was handsome and she wondered if he was as vicious as some of his tribe had been toward them. It did not matter she had fallen in love with him and words had never been passed between them. She saw a kindness in his eyes and they betrayed the cruelties of a warrior. She knew in her heart he would never hurt her.

The warrior returned to the mountaintop and looked for her. He had slipped away from his tribe unnoticed and hopefully he would be able to return before they knew he was missing. His eyes scanned the area looking intently for her, but she was not there. Disappointed, he began to head back toward his village. Just as he rounded a bend ahead of him he spotted what he thought to be a glimpse of her dress in the forest. Carefully, he walked around the glen and found her sitting on a log staring out across the valley.

What happened from this point is a private matter, but from that day forward they spent every moment they could together, praying they would not be caught by others. Each day they were away from each other seemed an eternity. Their hearts cried out for each other at night.

Tempers rose high within the tribes and a great battle was soon to be fought between them. The young warrior was told that when the red of the sun began to rise in the sky the battle would begin. He met with his lover on that morning at the rock and declared his love for her. She in turn promised her heart to him for all to see. He told her of the battle and of his fear of never seeing her again. In his sorrow, he decided to throw himself from the mountaintop. He would rather be dead than have to bear being without her.

The warrior slipped from her arms and jumped from the overhanging rock. She prayed for the Great Spirit to bring him back to her. The mighty winds rising from the gorge lifted the warrior high into the air and delivered him back to the spot from where he had jumped.

This legend does not give us any hope as to the young lovers ever being able to live together for the rest of their lives. It does not give us the outcome of the great battle between the Cherokee and the Catawba. It does give us the power of prayer and the powers of the Great Spirit. If the legend is to be believed, we will know the warrior and his lover may still be together somewhere in eternity.

The Devil's Staircase

Thousands of places in North America and around the world have places believed to be haunted by Satan himself. There are tales of caves, houses, mansions... buildings of every type and description can be found bearing the mark of Satan. Whether it is a place for him to be worshipped or a place for his minions and followers to do their deeds, you will find them everywhere.

With the schedule this entity keeps, it is a small wonder how so many places in the state of North Carolina can have something named for the devil: The Devil's Tramping Ground in Siler City, the Devil's Tower, Devil's Den, just to name a few. All of these places have legends of being haunted or have sightings of strange and often frightening phenomena. Footsteps, voices from beyond, and the icy touch of something from the grave are just a few of the things these places have in common.

Ashe County, North Carolina, has its very own claim to fame for something belonging to Satan. Early in the twentieth century, a road through the mountains was built for residents and travelers to be able to traverse the mountains between North Carolina and Tennessee. It is North Carolina Highway 88. At the bend of the river, a site was dynamited to make way for the new road. It gives the appearance of a staircase turned upside down. A black construction worker was killed here during the building of the road; the manner in which he died has been blamed on him being too close to a dynamite blast. His death is still remembered and it is believed that his spirit is part of the area's haunting. The voice of a man can be heard when there is nobody around.

Another tale told of this place may be disturbing to those with a conscience: it's claimed a woman killed her unwanted child here. The reasons are unknown other than she had no desire to keep the child.

The most popular legends for the Devil's Stairs concerns phantom riders. Drivers passing the Devil's Stairs have looked into their rearview mirrors to see an unknown passenger riding in the backseat — and they say it was Satan himself riding with them.

From the sightings reported, it has been agreed that the face of the phantom rider is hidden. His features are hooded in a cloak of black, making him appear very ominous and mysteriously quiet.

The tale of a phantom rider can be found in every culture and state. The description is usually the same, but it is seldom that you hear about Satan himself hitching a ride with you in the lonely hours of darkness. This makes the area of Highway 88 unique in its own right. The vision of large stairs and a dark and lonely night in an area where pedestrians are not to be seen can be an unnerving experience for the faint of heart.

If you should venture to the "Devil's Staircase," you may encounter a ghostly rider accompanying you on your travels. However, do not fear... They will soon reach their destination and leave you to your prayers.

The Legend of Tijuana Fats

The sleepy little town of Blowing Rock, North Carolina, brings back the days of past with wonderful clarity. The indisputable charm of its shaded sidewalks and shops will bring you back time and time again just to visit and talk with residents and shopkeepers.

The population of the town is small, but it carries a heart as big as the Carolina skies. Blowing Rock is located in both Watauga and Caldwell counties and is within a stone's throw of Boone. This small mountain oasis has been an alluring attraction for visitors for more than 150 years.

Perched on this mountainside, the years have seen boarding houses and home rentals that were a place of rest for thousands. The restaurants of the area today boast many fine foods and wines to delight. You will be entertained with music while talking with local artisans as you pass the day.

Some years ago a lady purchased a building on Main Street in historic downtown Blowing Rock. The site was perfect for her new restaurant venture. She looked forward to each and every day serving her guests and the residents of Blowing Rock. Shortly after she opened her new business, she began to notice that some of the employees seemed nervous about going into certain areas of the restaurant. The timing was never the same, but the area was always the exact spot. The history of the building noted that it was once a residence as well as a boutique.

The new owner was not curious by nature, but she had an eye for detail and many things never went unnoticed. The front windows of the establishment locked securely with solid latches. There appeared to be no breeze allowed in, but at times the chandeliers in one of the dining areas would swing on their own accord. The curious thing was they did not swing back and forth, but in circles.

The owner attributed the movement to an odd breeze coming through cracks in the window casings. She carried on her duties as though nothing was amiss, but before long guests began to mention seeing a small child in the hallway. When approached, she disappeared behind the curtain. The child did seem friendly and they all wondered about her presence.

The sightings and odd situations began to escalate with both employees and guests. Some were thrilled to witness something from another time or the unexplained. Others just passed the happenings off as though everything was normal. The apparition of the child was far from normal. She usually appeared at the most inconvenient times for the employees. The child was usually dressed from a period dating back to the late 1800s or the very early 1900s, and was noted to have pretty blond hair with ringlets and a penchant for playing tricks on her host.

The former home of Tijuana Fats and the ghost of little Mary.

The child was seen often by employees at closing time when the back closet was used the most. This closet held supplies and also led to a rear entrance through another door. The back door was securely locked from the inside with no possible way for anyone to come and go through the door. Often, the squeaking of the hinges was heard as though someone was opening or closing doors. This doubled the enigma of who the child actually was and how she was escaping them. It was said the building caught fire when it was used as a residence. A young child named Mary may have lost her life and has since returned to haunt the building.

The middle dining room was the most pleasant place for diners to enjoy themselves and it was affectionately called "Mary's Room." There sits an aged fireplace from another place and time. The slate footing of the fireplace is marked with the footprint of a small child. Where and when the footprint first appeared cannot be determined. The remarkable thing is this footprint is imbedded in the slate!

Another of Mary's playful tricks were to turn on the faucets in the kitchen; however, if you asked nicely, she would turn them off for you. It was not unusual to find the bar glasses to be perfectly lined up along the bar when the staff entered to open the restaurant in the morning. Mary did not show herself to everyone, but when she did make an appearance it is one you were not likely to forget.

The atmosphere within these walls was not discomforting and one could relax and enjoy themselves with ease. There is something about sitting at your table by the fireplace that will bring back nostalgic feelings. Tijuana Fats is no longer, but for twenty years Mary was the star attraction for all who came to know and love her.

The footprint of a small child embedded in slate by the fireplace.

6

Haywood County

In the 1700s, the Cherokees allied with the British and 2,400 troops were led against the rebelling Cherokees from Haywood County. These men were led by General Griffith Rutherford. At the end of the war, the men returned to Haywood County and continued their lives. The county consists of four towns closely placed together; the most famous of these towns is Maggie Valley, which did not incorporate until 1974.

Pisgah

Within the far reaches of Haywood County, bordering on Buncombe County, is Mount Pisgah. Reverend George Newton, a teacher in Western North Carolina during the eighteenth century, is credited for naming the mountain. This area is renowned for its beauty. Visitors from all over the world come to see Pisgah for its panoramic views. Pisgah is a biblical name meaning the Promised Land. This is exactly as the European settlers saw this place: one of great beauty. With the bounty of game and lush forest, they sat in awe of its majesty.

Pisgah was once the land of the Cherokee and it belonged to no other. The Catawba Indians and all others respected this. The land that is now the property of the state was also once the site of a hunting lodge belonging to George Vanderbilt. It was named Buck Springs Lodge and built around the turn of the twentieth century. The remains of the lodge are still there for all to see.

The Cherokee had well developed routes for traveling through the countryside for trading as well as other uses. A short distance from the remains of the former Vanderbilt lodge is a wide path intersecting with what is now known as the Pisgah parking area. This large parking area offers panoramic views with places for the weary traveler to relax. Just off the Blue Ridge Parkway, it is very easy to locate.

The backside of the parking area is the remnants of the former Cherokee trail used for their travels, as well as a refuge at night. It shelters you from the cold night winds that travel through the mountains. Camping here they were able to see all around them even in the darkness of night. The Cherokee also believed it was protected by spirits. They felt the safety of the camp was never in jeopardy due to the protection of these spirits. Their enemies would not be able to find them.

Visiting this part of the old trail you will get the distinct feeling that you are not alone. There is a tranquil feeling to this narrow road as inviting as you could ever ask for. It invites comfort to your senses in its own way. You can actually feel the presence of

A portion of the former road used by the Cherokee and other tribes to travel through the mountains.

something (for lack of a better word) there with you. Whispers in the night are not uncommon and travelers have reported seeing apparitions on the path.

The legends may be justifiably true. The Cherokee have traveled this path for as long as anyone can remember and know the area well. It is their words that ring through time with the declaration of the guardian spirits. It is said you will never be harmed as long as you are true of heart and virtue when you are here.

Over the years photographs taken of the path have produced some unusual results. One such photograph produced an image that makes it uncertain as to whether an actual spirit was captured or not. The path appeared to be clear of trees or other obstructions at the time, and yet through the darkness a face appeared in the photograph with peculiar characteristics. This photograph was taken in the presence of four witnesses who declare there was nothing to see when the picture was taken other than total darkness. The face is surrounded by total darkness in the center of the path! It is possible this could be one of the guardian spirits the Cherokee had spoken of.

Investigators in the field of the paranormal have researched the area and found several anomalies. One of the investigations produced what they believe to be the presence of spirits. It is believed spirits will draw energy from objects such as batteries when they are present. They use this energy for their own purposes, such as trying to manifest. At one point, the five investigators stood discussing their next point in the investigation. It was then they realized every battery they had in their equipment was totally drained at the same time. Their cell phone batteries had been drained also. One investigator discovered he could no longer use his camera. It refused to work. He thought it was due to battery drain. This was not the case. No sooner than he left the area the camera worked perfectly.

The Cherokee say the spirits here are not to be disturbed. It is possible the spirits felt their presence as an intrusion and made themselves known. There was no disrespect intended in their investigation, yet it is still frowned upon to disturb them.

The spirits of this land are still vigilant and want visitors to feel the safety of their home. As the Cherokee say: "Show respect in all things and you will be welcomed."

Animal Spirits

Hunters have killed and butchered animals for their meat for as long as man has been on the face of the Earth. You have read the stories of people, in biblical times, killing sheep and cows to feed their families. The killing of animals for survival is nothing new. The killing of animals for sport or a trophy is fairly modern. The laws of nature dictate you should never kill for the sake of killing...you should do this for survival only. The Cherokee offer up a small prayer and ask for the life of the animal before it is taken for meat.

It is the respect for this, as in all things, that they offer these prayers for the blessing. There are animals in the forest that should never be killed. They are the spirits of others who have passed from this life and returned to guide us in animal form. The belief is so strong that many friendships have been lost for the sake of the belief.

These animals always have an appearance, such as coloration, or distinctive spots, letting you know who they are. You may find a deer, solid white or black in color. As a hunter, you already know this is not a normal deer. It is believed it is the spirit of someone who has returned.

When a young warrior or anyone in the tribe passes from this world, he does not die. He returns to us from the spirit world to protect and guide us through our lives. Many times he will do this in the form of an animal. This is not a superstition; it is a belief that is sacred for many even today.

In the late 1990s, a small group of men left their homes to meet for a bear hunt. They had hunted together for many years and were the best of friends. Three of the men in the party were from the Cherokee Nation. The others were white men of European descent. They always ate what they killed; it was never for sport.

This trip was to be different. By the end of the hunt the Cherokee would no longer be friends with the men they had known for so many years. It was the second hunt of the season and the dogs used for tracking the bears were pulling at their leashes, eager to start the hunt. The men had set up camp in the valley and planned where they wanted to start the hunt. They knew the bear in this area were supposed to be plentiful this year. Each man made certain their guns were ready and they had everything they needed. The next morning they rose from their sleeping bags at daybreak and cooked their breakfast over the open flames of the camp fire.

Within the hour they had already breached the waters of a nearby creek where bear were known to feed. They found nothing but a few old tracks. Delving deeper into the foliage and headed up the ridge, the dogs broke scent on a very large bear. The sounds of the dogs running the bear echoed through the gorge. This sound was a hunter's delight. The dogs tried to tree the bear three times, but the bear was able to escape them before the hunters could reach their dogs.

Four hours into the hunt, the hounds cornered the black bear in an outcrop of rocks. The hunters made their way to the sounds of the dogs fighting with the bear. From the size of his tracks he would weigh about three hundred pounds. This was exciting news! The great bear became visible as they rounded the outcropping. Each hunter took a stand in place, not only for his own protection but also in order to get a shot at the bear. Suddenly, the bear stood tall on his legs and the hunters could see a large patch of white fur in the center of his chest. One of the men brought his rifle to bear on the great beast and fired before anything could be said. The Cherokees never attempted to raise their guns in an effort to kill the bear. All of this occurred within a scant few minutes. The Cherokee found it hard to believe their friend had killed this bear.

The hunters examined their kill with the other men talking of never seeing such a bear before in all their years of hunting. When they returned to camp, the stories went around the fire of other animals with strange markings. The Cherokee in their own way tried to tell the hunter he had made a mistake by killing the bear. He should ask for forgiveness from the Great Spirit. Their warnings went unheeded.

The Cherokee stayed faithful to their beliefs that the bear that was hunted and killed was a spirit bear and should have never been hunted. The white men scoffed at the idea and not only relished their trophy, but displayed its head in homes and other places.

The friends who had hunted together for so many years were no longer friends. Their fellow hunters had encroached on a sacred belief. The Cherokee do not hunt game with these men any longer, nor do they speak with each other when they meet. There are some beliefs that are not to be denied even for the sake of friendship.

Francis

There are hundreds of colorful stories and legends to be told by our older generation. They were weaned on some of the finest folklore ever to be found in the mountains of North Carolina. From the whimsical stories of pranksters to the ghostly legend, there was never a dull moment. Some were just tall tales for the children's entertainment while others had an endearing quality to touch the heart of the listener.

In this life, we all have things we love dearly. A man can become easily attached to an animal. It is a sort of kinship that cannot be explained. The animal returns this affection in ways that are readily recognizable to people outside of his realm. The loyalty of the animal to the master is unmistakable even to a stranger.

In a time long past, farmers used mules to tend their crops, pull their heavily laden wagons, or just ride to town when they had no desire to walk. A good mule was almost more valuable than a male child born into a family.

Haywood County is best known for vacation fun and relaxation. It offers mountain music and delicacies to delight even the most discriminating taste buds, especially Maggie Valley. It lies a mere fifteen miles from the Cherokee reservation via Soco Road. In the hills surrounding Maggie Valley lived a farmer called Hezzie. This was short for Hezekia. He was a mild-mannered man who believed in doing good for everyone. Hezzie was generous almost to a fault. He gladly helped his friends and neighbors in their times of need, although, at times, his assistance would leave him in a time of need. He never complained, but endured any hardship he placed upon himself.

Hezzie's prize possession was a white mule named Francis... Francis would walk through the farm with him, even on the days when Hezzie had nothing for her to do. They were almost inseparable. In the evening, Francis would not stay in the stable as most animals did. She would open the gate with her nose and stand ready by the window of Hezzie's home. Francis loved Hezzie more than life itself. She protected him from snakes and other creatures roaming the land, nuzzling his shoulder softly when he seemed troubled. You knew when Hezzie was coming down the road. The sound you heard first was the hooves of Francis and then shortly you would see Hezzie with Francis at his shoulder.

Hezzie came to town one afternoon to purchase some cloth and a few other things for his wife. Francis was nowhere to be seen. Neighbors inquired as to where Francis could be. With a tear in his eye, Hezzie told them Francis had passed into the arms of the Lord that very morning. Seeing Hezzie without Francis was not a pleasant thing. It was as though Hezzie's very life had been drained from his body. He no longer stood shoulders back or had a brisk gait to his walk. Now, he just trodded along the road like a man lost in the wilderness.

Some years went by and Hezzie was not seen as much as before. Neighbors who usually saw him in town had to visit the farm to talk with him. He was frail and thin with little to say. He no longer smiled. His wife said Hezzie was grieving over Francis.

Hezzie became ill and lay in his bed barely able to raise his head. His wife tended his needs and prayed for his strength to return. One morning, she walked into his bedroom to bring him some breakfast. Glancing out of the bedroom window, she could have sworn she glimpsed a white mule by the corner of the barn. Shaking her head, she just passed it off as an old memory. While washing the dishes after his breakfast, she heard the sound of hooves slowly passing the kitchen window. Thinking it was a neighbor coming to check on Hezzie, she called out. There was no answer and there was nobody in the yard.

Hezzie's wife was no fool. She thought about the things that were beginning to happen around her home. When she hung her freshly laundered clothes on the line outside to dry, sometimes Francis would pull Hezzie's work shirt from the line. Lately, each time she hung the clothes to dry she would return to find Hezzie's shirt on the ground. Only Francis could have done this. She decided to dress Hezzie one fine morning and put his work shoes on him. This may be a way to make him want to leave his bed. Searching for his work shoes, she found them inside of the stall Hezzie had for Francis.

Hezzie's wife began to wonder if she was losing her mind. She wrote to her sister and asked her to come and visit for awhile and help her take care of Hezzie. Her sister agreed and arrived within a week of her letter. The sightings of Francis increased, with her sister seeing the mule almost everyday. The sound of Francis walking near the house was plain for all to hear. Soon, word reached into the valley, and others came to possibly see and hear Francis.

Hezzie awoke just after lunch a few days before Christmas. He sat erect in the bed to the amazement of everyone. He talked of old times and what he wanted to do. His eyes turned to the window and asked if Francis had been fed on that day. Thinking Hezzie was losing his mind, they all agreed Francis was well-taken care of. Hearing this, Hezzie lay back down and closed his eyes. He never spoke another word. On Christmas morning, Hezzie left this world to the sadness of all those who loved him.

People who cared for Hezzie came to call and give their condolences to his family. One of the visitors asked when he had bought another mule. His wife was quick to tell them he had not and what he most likely saw was Francis. The visitor inquired as to what convinced her to believe this. She told him the mule started coming back after Hezzie had become bedridden. She was not the only one to see Francis and knew it could be no other mule than Francis for the things that were happening.

Shaking his head in disbelief, this visitor left the house and headed for his home. While crossing the yard, he distinctly heard the sound of a mule's heavy trod coming up behind him. He turned quickly and saw the yard behind him was empty.

Hezzie was to be buried in the cemetery of the local Baptist church. On the day of the funeral, the entire community came to see him once again before he would seek his eternal rest. The sermon being over, Hezzie's pallbearers carried him from the church and placed his casket in the back of a neighbor's truck to be taken to his grave. As the truck headed for his last resting place, the sound of hooves accompanied them all the way to the gravesite. As the mourners turned away from the grave, Hezzie's wife turned to her sister, "I guess that old mule came to see him off proper." Her sister nodded in agreement, "Yes, I heard her walking all the way to his grave."

It would be pleasant to think an animal loved her master so dearly she came back to say good-bye... Did she?

7

Cleveland County

Cleveland County was formed in 1841. It was named for Colonel Benjamin Cleveland, who fought in the great battles at King's Mountain; these battles turned the tide of the Revolutionary War and forced the British to retreat to South Carolina.

Located in the Piedmont of the southwestern portion in the foothills of the Blue Ridge Mountains, the county harbors mountains on one side and wide beaches on the other. This makes Cleveland County a desirable place for businesses as well as those who are family-oriented. This county also holds ghostly tales that leave little to the imagination.

King's Mountain

Yorktown, Concord, Bennington, and Saratoga... These are the places the average person thinks of when you mention the Revolutionary War. This war of independence was fought in many places, especially in the southern part of the United States. The Continental Army was led by such generals as George Washington in the North and Nathaniel Greene in the South. Horatio Gates later took command of the Continental troops in the South.

General Cornwallis sent his troops in to defeat the colonists and nearly succeeded. However, thanks to the efforts of strong-willed American troops, General Cornwallis was soundly defeated at almost every turn in the South.

In the beginning, Cornwallis defeated the troops in Georgia and South Carolina, placing them beneath his rule. This was short-lived for the British. At the Battle of King's Mountain on October 7, 1780, the left wing of the British Army was totally defeated with a massive loss of troops — the loss was so great that the troops withdrew and reformed in Wilmington, North Carolina, for resupply. They made their next advance into Virginia, unable to conquer North Carolina.

King's Mountain borders both North and South Carolina with its battlefields still intact for Americans to see. This battle caused the loss of life for twenty-eight loyal colonists. The British and the Loyalists to the crown lost 225 men, with 716 men captured. This would be a devastating blow to any enemy, not to mention the embarrassment to Lord Cornwallis.

Due to the ferocity of the colonists, the British suffered this defeat at the hands of soldiers aging from a mere ten years old to the age of fifty. These were seasoned veterans fighting on their home ground against a power said to be undefeatable. The battle went down in history as one of our finest hours. Today, when you visit King's Mountain and tour the National Park dedicated to these brave men, pay close attention to what may be happening around you.

When the battle ended, the dead were buried as they were on the battlefield in unmarked graves. The serenity of King's Mountain is much like the lull before the storm. The dead never rest in an unmarked grave. It is possible they may feel forgotten for the sacrifice they made for their country. This we will never know, but be assured that these soldiers do *not* rest. They have not given up the battle and make their presence known to others today.

Visitors to the battlefield in Cleveland County have reported sighting troops on horseback as well as soldiers of the infantry. They have asked the rangers if there will be a re-enactment on the grounds later in the day. This question has become so prevalent that the rangers have, reportedly, started ignoring the inquiry. These sightings have been happening for many years and are not just a recent phenomena.

The sightings of these soldiers are hard to believe for the average person. Nonetheless, the sightings were not confined to a single person, but appeared to groups of tourist that had come to visit the site of one of America's greatest battles. The tourists were able to describe with perfect clarity what the soldiers and their mounts looked like. The men's faces were like solid figures... just as the living who witnessed the events. Their packs, rifles, and everything about them held no unearthly qualities, which is why those who have witnessed the men question their presence. Some witnesses have reported seeing the men on more than one occasion in the same day!

Other areas of the United States have reported such specters on battlefields as well, with Gettysburg a very good example of this. In those cases, the soldiers normally were not clear to one's vision or held a peculiar quality to the lighting around them. Usually the soldier's feet cannot be seen or you can see objects through the entity because of a misty looking version of the man. Usually a full-bodied apparition is rare.

The witnesses to the events at King's Mountain have habitually reported something far greater. Some have not only seen the soldiers, but have also heard the sounds that accompany the men. The sound of boots moving through the forest mingled with the sounds of horses. It is not to be denied that at times people can use their imaginations to such an extent that they actually believe they have witnessed some unusual phenomena. Mass hallucination cannot be used in an effort to deny what these people have seen. Is it possible the rangers also have been induced to the imaginations of the visitors who no longer walk the grounds of the battlefield and park? Common sense would say no to this question. The rangers employed here have witnessed ghostly shapes and heard sounds of battle also.

The number of people claiming sightings is not small. We often wonder exactly what they were seeing or if they were just caught up in a moment of history. Whatever the case may be, there are times when the dead come back to us in a moment of what is known as a *residual haunting* — a massive bundle of energy mortals left as an imprint on time and space. These brave men need to know there sacrifice is not forgotten and we honor them for their service.

Rutherford County

A little-known fact concerning all these counties mentioned thus far is the number of very famous men who made history. Rutherford County residents are no stranger to this list of prestigious men also. Joshua Forman, the builder of the Erie Canal, was a long time resident here. Each and every county participated in the Revolutionary War with some of their residents becoming high-ranking officers.

Before the California gold rush, Rutherford County and North Carolina was home to the most gold mines in the entire country. In the mid-1880s through the 1890s, there was other gold to be made here. The award-winning movie *Dirty Dancing* was largely filmed here at Lake Lure. This is just a few of the wonderful moments in history for the people of Rutherford County, North Carolina.

Green River Plantation

T he picture a person conjures in his mind when the word "plantation" is mentioned varies greatly. The one thing all of these thoughts have in mind is a beautiful mansion filled with luxurious furniture and an air of southern aristocracy. The grounds are wonderfully shaded to create an oasis of respite from the heat and provide a place of beauty for their guests to rest themselves from the rigors of life.

The current owners here have turned the estate into an intriguing bed and breakfast. They welcome each and every person to come and visit with them. Weddings and beautifully set parties are often held here. The mansion is located in Rutherford County, North Carolina. Through the many hauntings and folklore passed down through the ages here, this plantation house is a must-see.

On the living room wall there is said to hang a portrait of two very large black dogs. No doubt these would be the valued pets of a former owner of the estate. Many times prized animals were painted in portraits to honor them after they passed. Visitors of the estate have had the experience of seeing at least one of the animals roaming the grounds. The dog has been known to growl at more than one unsuspecting visitor. They learn later of the painting and then the date of the painting. The date is 1787 — the dog they encountered has been dead for more than two hundred years — yet they all say it was the exact same dog.

Not far from the back door of the plantation house is a small tombstone. The carvings are brief and barely discernable, but none-the-less readable. It simply reads: "Infant 1803." The identity of the child has not been discovered. It has somehow slipped through the pages of the mansion's history without notice. The child is certainly not forgotten, as people have heard the distinct cry of a baby. A search for the sound always brings forth no discovery of an infant on the property. The people who have heard the sound of the baby wailing swear they were not hearing things. After all, the women who have heard this are mothers themselves and there is no mistaking the cry of an infant.

Quite often the ghosts of Green River revel in making themselves known. Objects are moved in the night to the wonderment of others occupying the building. Small objects may become unnoticeable, but the stacking of chairs is something one can only show amazement. After the mansion has closed for the night, one wonders who has inhabited the home. Speculation has led to many areas, but never to one single source. Some believe it is the spirit of a black slave that worked in this home long ago.

The average plantation did have slaves. It must be noted here that all slaves were not treated badly, especially in the State of North Carolina. Most slaves, after a few years, became land owners due to the generosity of some of those who owned slaves. They would be free men and were given land for their families to farm and in some cases became partners of their former owners. Mankind creates strange friendships and those who have become friends through the worst of times usually are closer than anyone can imagine. The number of former slaves that stayed on plantations after the War Between the States was surprising. Many stayed on as sharecroppers, holding various other jobs, including overseers of the property they once worked.

Behind the Green Park Plantation house once stood the quarters for the slaves. The house is long gone now, but one of the residents is not finished here. Dressed in the style of the 1800s, a black woman has been seen walking toward the back of the house. Though she looks as real as you or me, she hurries toward the house as if she has many things to do. Some people, thinking she may be an re-enactor, have tried speaking with her, but their only response was silence as she hurried on and then disappeared before their eyes once she reached the back-door of the plantation. The owners told them they have no actors on the premises and wonder what they have seen.

This specter is not bound to just crossing the yard of the back of the house. She is also seen in the house, close to where the kitchen is located. It is here that she disappears through the wall and out of the back of the house.

A visit to this wonderful Bed and Breakfast is as pleasant to the eye as it is to the palate. I am sure your experience here will create a treasure of pleasant memories for the years to come.

9

Sevier County

Sevier County, Tennessee, is bordered on the south by the state of North Carolina. The other boundary for the Great Valley of East Tennessee are the states of Georgia and Virginia. Two rivers join to make the Tennessee River: the French Broad River and the Holston River. It is known to the residents as "The Forks." From the great heights of Clingman's Dome, this amazing sight is easily seen.

The county was formed in 1794 and covers six hundred square miles of some of the most beautiful sights to be found in nature. The centerpiece for the courthouse that was constructed in 1895 is a clock built by the famous Seth Thomas at a cost of $1,300 — it is still in perfect working order. It stands at the center of a 130-foot tower. Those who know clocks best have labeled this work of art as "flawless."

The Healing Place

The waters of the Oconoluftee River rush westward, reaching deep into the Smokey Mountains of North Carolina. Its crystal clear waters form a border separating North Carolina from its neighbor, Tennessee. The State has designated the mountain that overlooks the Oconoluftee as Clingman's Dome. However, the Cherokee, as well as the White man, know it as the "Gall Place."

Beneath a clear blue sky, people stand in wonderment as they gaze across a landscape where seven states can be seen. The beautiful peaks and valleys are settled before them unlike anything they may witness in a lifetime. The sight is never the same, as each day the mountains change with the sunrise. It's as though the hand of God has brought before you a very special gift.

For longer than anyone can remember, this dome has harbored a great secret. The Cherokee came here to pray and ask for the blessing from Mother Earth, that she would help them with their lives. They needed the balance to be as one with the spiritual self, as well as live in harmony with their surroundings. You must live peacefully with the animals in the forest as well as the trees, earth, and waters that supply food and shelter for the families. This, they, and others, believe; and this practice of harmony within nature continues to this day. The spirits walk here and pass the things they have learned when they walked among us.

When a man has fasted and prayed, he waits for his prayers to be answered. If he is worthy, and his heart is pure, the magic lake will appear before him in the valley beneath him. He may then come forth to cleanse himself in its waters and be healed. From this moment on, he will be one with everything the Great One has placed before him because he is pure of heart.

Those who say they have witnessed the lake speak of the nearly impossible journey it would take for a man to reach it. Others say it can and has been done, but only by the few that have been truly blessed. The bear and the deer that have been

Over look from Clingman's Dome of the valley where the magic lake appears.

wounded by the hunter's bow can come to the healing place when they need to. They do not come to die or seek solace from the world outside. They come to be healed and they always are. Birds fly freely in great flocks for all to see without fear of man over the waters of the lake.

People come to visit Clingman's Dome by the thousands each year, to see the view of the mountain range spread for many miles before them. They read the story of the Magic Lake and pass it off as just a myth created by man. It is a place of healing whether you believe the story or not. Once you have descended from the dome and continued on your journey, you may recall the story, never realizing your life has changed by merely gazing upon the majesty of the valley below.

10

Graham County

G raham County retains its charm and beauty by being partly isolated. The forming of the county was slow in development because of the rugged conditions men were forced to work with. This county is well-known for its category four and five rapids, which kayakers revel in for only seventeen days out of the year, depending on how much water is released from the nearby dams.

Graham County formed in 1872 from a portion of Cherokee County. Once they did, it became easier to enforce the law and make courts more uniform. It is part of the Great Smoky Mountains with the Unicoi range running from the western boundary between Graham County and Tennessee. The Snowbird Mountains run between the Unicoi Mountains and Red Marble Gap at the western entrance to the Nantahala Gorge.

The Little People

The Cherokee as well as the Whites have believed in the existence of a small race of people inhabiting the mountains of Western North Carolina for centuries. Long before the first White settler came to these lands, the Little People have made themselves known to the Cherokee people.

There are believed to be three races or clans of the Little People, or the Yun'ni Tsunsdi,' as they are called by the Cherokee nation. The belief is strong and not just a story to scare children or adults. They speak in an ancient dialect of the Cherokee, Elati, now considered extinct. Some say there are elders of the tribe who still speak and can understand a language that has long-since been out of use by the tribe.

Since the first written records, as well as in oral traditions, Cherokee medicine men have visited the Little People for their secrets of healing those who are ill. These healers of the tribe would venture deep into the mountains to ask for their help in healing the Cherokee people. The trek was long and never easy. They would stay with the Little People for a period of seven days and seven nights. During this time, they were given secret medicines for their tribe while the Cherokee taught them the prayers, the songs of the bear, and dances that would aid the Little People in their lives. At the end of one year, the medicine men were to return the secrets. They honored their agreement and, one by one, the secrets were returned.

The Little People have been called dwarfs and midgets. A dwarf is disproportionate in body. The Little People are not; they are perfectly formed in stature and physique. The ones who have interacted with the Cherokee have been described as short of stature, between two to four feet in height. They are known to dress the same as the Cherokee. Their coal black hair is usually long enough that it almost touches the ground. They do not want to be disturbed in any way. It is well known that they will usually appear at dusk or the dawning of the day. They are only seen when they wish to be seen.

Accordingly, in their interaction with the Cherokee and some Whites, it has been noted that they can be very helpful in all matters. It is for you to ask. Yet they must be respected. The Little People are said to have never been born and they will never die.

Of the three clans of Little People you have the Rock People, who are known to be mean or spiteful when their domain has been invaded; the Laurel People, who are mischievous and love to play pranks on people; and the Dogwood, who is reported to be good and like to care for people. It is also shown to be a great respect to not speak of the Little People after dark.

An example of the respect that must be shown toward the Little People or face their wrath is a story told by the mother of Eddie L. After visiting some friends, he was headed for his home a few miles from Goose Creek. When he reached Adams Creek, he decided to take a short-cut across the mountain his father had shown him. Much to his surprise, when he attempted

The end of this drive lays the beginning of the path taken by Eddie the night he encountered the Rock People in the 1946.

to broach the path, a small man sat on a large rock and hissed a warning not to come any further. Eddie was young and strong and would not stand for this small creature telling him where he could go. Reaching down, he gathered some stones and threw them with all his might at the little man sitting perched upon the large rock. The stones found their mark, but they had no effect on the little man. He sneered viciously at Eddie and left the rock in the blink of an eye.

Eddie arrived home later than expected and his father questioned him concerning his timing. He explained to his father what had happened and what his actions were. His father swore vehemently and told his son he had offended one of the Little People and he now feared for his safety. Eddie scoffed at his father's words, telling him he would not be bothered by a little man. He feared nothing. Later that night Eddie ascended the stairs and put himself to bed for the night. He felt slightly disoriented and thought he had exerted himself too much during the day with his friends.

One of the many areas said to belong to the Little People of the Cherokee.

Eddie's father worried for his son and decided to watch over him during the night. In the wee hours of the morning, his father heard a sound coming from the upstairs that was out of the ordinary. It was neither a loud noise nor was it a disturbing one. He went up the stairs to see what had caused the heavy rustling sound on the bare board of the flooring. He found his son just in time... His body was halfway out through the window yet his feet never touched the floor! On top of that, the young man was still sleeping! The fall would have broken his neck without a doubt. This happened in the summer of 1946. In the days after the incident, Eddie left gifts for the little man in an attempt to apologize for his behavior. In the same breath, he asked for his forgiveness.

Today, as you visit the mountains of Western North Carolina, you may notice there are fences built on some of the properties that seem to be incomplete. Those who believe in the Little People build their fences leaving a small space in the fence for the Little People to be able to pass without hindrance.

The Little People live in small caves within the mountains. Should you encounter one of the Little People, respect their space and speak to them with kindness. Should you or your child become lost in these mountains your very salvation may lay in the kindness of the Little People?

Soldier's Crossing

The Cherohala Skyway is a series of twists and turns taking you through the Tellico Plains with vistas you are not likely to ever forget. The days are pleasant, even in the cold of winter. Clear, star-filled skies overhead will make you forget the rigors of life with their beauty. This region of Western North Carolina can take you back before the time of the automobile without having to close your eyes. Each road taken off the beaten path bears reminders of the days long past.

In the 1700s, the Cherokee and the White man traveled through the hills taking long-forgotten paths to make their way into Tennessee for trading and other business. Battles were fought between the Indian nations to settle disputes of all kinds throughout the area. The travelers and settlers of this region often fished the Tellico River and used it for traveling at times. Lake Santeetla bore the ageless footprints of centuries of explorers to the region.

The Skyway itself is not old in years, but the history of the area is to be envied for its uses when America was a fledgling nation. The lands belonged to the Cherokee at the time and were known as the "Over Hill Cherokee" to the settlers of Tennessee. This was the Unicoi Mountain Range. Trading across the border was a trek that involved crossing twenty-four steep mountains and trails. There were settlements dotting the landscape with dozens of farms and villages belonging to the Cherokee.

In the Robbinsville area of Graham County, there were middle towns — Tassetchee, Elijay, and Nequassee — or multi-phase sites that had periods of being populated dating back thousands of years. These sites are still being excavated today by archeologists.

The trail used by the Cherokee and the Europeans was known as the Wachesa Trail. It led from Murphy, North Carolina, toward Beaverdam Creek and began its descent to Unicoi Gap and Coker Creek. Today, the Joe Brown Highway follows the old trail to a great extent.

A short few miles from the turn-off for the village of Snowbird is a cutback leading to a clearing now used as a burial ground. The road runs all the way through the cemetery back to Tellico Road. This is not a thoroughfare, but a means to have more than one route to the burial grounds. In many years past, there were no graves here, but near the back of the plot is a stand of trees consisting of a mix of Pine and hardwood trees. Seeing this you can still barely make the essence of an old path once used by people crossing here behind the tree line.

The Cherokee, Europeans, and Spanish soldiers were also said to have crossed here while traveling across the mountains. During the Civil War, soldiers were ambushed along the mountain range by snipers or small groups of men. There were times that men who were not even fighting in the war were killed...these were innocent civilians who happened to be at the wrong place. Robbers and thieves were not unknown as well, but rarely was anyone killed for the price of their goods.

The story of the spirit of three soldiers is not a new one, though when it all began is unclear at best. There are those who say these soldiers are the spirits of Spaniards while others say they are soldiers from the War Between the States. It has never been said they were Cherokee or warriors of a neighboring Indian tribe.

The legend states one of the first sightings was in the late 1800s by a hunter stalking deer. He came to rest against a large oak tree directly across from the small stand of trees by the clearing. Exhausted from the hunt, he took a short nap before venturing on. When he awoke, darkness was approaching so he

Fifteen yards from the tree is the entrance to part of an old path where soldiers are said to appear and cross to the woods on the other side of the burial ground.

decided he would camp there for the night because crossing the mountains in darkness was a fool's venture. He built his fire and cooked a meager meal as he watched the shadows play among the trees around him. He had hunted for game in this area for many years and knew it well. There was nothing to fear. Lighting his pipe he stared up at the stars and let his mind wander pleasantly for awhile. By his best guess, it was nearly 8 o'clock in the evening when he decided to go to sleep for the night.

He was clearly awake when he spotted what appeared to be a small light emerging from the stand of trees across from him. As he watched, the light appeared to separate and become three lights. Not knowing if he was in danger or not, he grabbed his rifle and stood behind the large Oak. The lights grew brighter. The lights did not come toward him as he thought they would. Instead they gathered in strength until the hunter could make out the figures of three men who appeared to be wearing uniforms. Their rifles and boots could be seen plainly from his vantage point. Their faces appeared anonymous, indistinct of features. The three soldiers never looked his way or attempted to go toward him. Instead they headed for the far side of the clearing, stopping just short of the tree line.

The hunter watched them closely. They appeared to be talking to each other. Slowly, one of the soldiers turned from the group and crouched as if he had heard something. Without a sound, the three soldiers dissolved into thin air...leaving the hunter alone in the dark of night. Thinking back of the wonder he had seen, he remembered none of the soldiers wore a hat. The uniforms were plain as far as he could tell, as were their rifles. Everything about them made no sense as to what the hunter had witnessed.

Returning home, he told his friend what he had seen and soon found he was not the only person who had witnessed the soldiers. It was a rare sight indeed, but had been seen by more than a handful of men. All of the witnesses have reported different stories of the sighting, though they all agree on one point: the three men are soldiers. From what era, though, has never been determined. The witnesses question what happened for them to go to a particular spot and then disappear from sight. It has never been recorded that any soldiers were either ambushed or killed here or that anything out of the ordinary ever happened to cause these men to appear to others.

This sighting is rare and those who are lucky enough to witness the crossing of the soldiers may one day have some clue as to who they are. Until then it will remain another mystery of the Unicoi.

11

Clay County

I n 1837, General Winfield Scott was given the order to imprison the Cherokees and hold them in forts before transporting them to Oklahoma. One mile southwest of Hayesville, Captain Hembree built two small stockades to hold them. The Cherokee were known as one of the "Five Civilized Tribes." Fort Hembree was the official beginning of The Trail of Tears. The site of these forts can be found today in the Hayesville city limits.

Although the county was created in 1861, it held no organization or formal government until 1868. The majority of Clay County lies within the boundaries of the Nantahala National Forest. The Fire Creek Bear Reserve is located north of Tusquitee.

Time Stands Still

On the border of the Fires Creek Bear Reserve, you will find the beautiful Tusquitee Mountain Range. The community of Tusquitee is also located here among these mountains of Clay County; created in 1861, Clay County's first White settler built his businesses and home here in 1870. That settler was none other than Mr. John Covington Moore, and a place of honor is still held for him today when you visit Tusquitee.

The word Tusquitee, like many other places in Western North Carolina, is a Cherokee word meaning "Where the dogs laugh." It refers to an old legend about two mud puppies walking on the trail talking and laughing with each other.

Time passed and slowly the town grew in size to become a recognized community. It was a peaceful place, but events in history say otherwise for some of the other residents of the area. This area was one that came to be known for the forts that held the Cherokee before the Trail of Tears.

Homes were built in the rural areas surrounding Tusquitee, where men and women farm the land to make a living for themselves. Game was plentiful and this also fed the families, as well as fishing the rivers and streams. An Englishman came to Tusquitee desiring to build a new life. Purchasing a plot of land four miles from the town, he built a home suitable for a future family with children to carry on his name.

Though he had never farmed before, the Englishman had a natural talent for growing crops. Soon, he expanded his holdings and owned a very sizeable farm. His wealth began to grow and, with it, the Englishman found a wife with whom to share his life. He enjoyed coming home to a fine supper and resting himself by the fireplace. Several children were born into the house. Life was as he thought it should be....

Things are not always as they seem, though. To the world outside, the family was happy and content. They smiled and visited others and were always the first to grace the front doors of the church. It was obvious to everyone that this was a true family.

Behind the closed doors of their home, however, was a much different story.

Word started to spread through the community that things were not as perfect as they seemed at this house. Loud quarreling had been heard as some passed their home. The Englishman felt what happened in his house was no business of others and should be kept that way. The cold of winter came early in 1885, with heavy snow chilling you to the very bone. It was barely possible to reach the barns of his property for feeding and caring of his animals. The fireplace barely roared from the heat trying to keep the house warm enough for them.

Being closed-in with each other, tempers flared and the Englishman fought with his wife. Again, he threatened her and made it plain the house and everything inside of it was his to do with as he pleased. The sound of their voices carried through the valley for neighbors to hear.

Others began to notice his wife sometimes had unexplained bruises and the children became withdrawn, no longer visiting with friends. The Englishman gained a hard line to his face and only spoke when he needed something. His wife appeared as though she was slowly wasting away, her sadness shown plainly on what was once such a lovely face.

The following year brought disaster to the community. The Englishman raced his carriage through the town at top speed headed for home. Everyone saw the anger on his face. Others thought he may be in trouble, so they gathered their horses and carts and followed him home. They arrived too late....

The carriage stood silently by the front doors of the home and not a sound was to be heard. The Englishman was found inside the house with a bullet to his head. The wife as well was laying on the floor where he had slain her in his fit of rage. As for the children, it was a blessing they were all away at the time of the murder.

In later years, the property was sold, but no one ever stayed for long in the Englishman's house. No reason was given, other than it being old and drafty. There are others who say different. Candlelights are seen in the windows of a house empty of a single, living soul. The sounds of voices are heard in the night, with not a soul to be seen.

In the early 1970s, three people ventured onto the property for their own reasons. They were there to spotlight deer. Illegal, by all means, but done just the same by more than one loving the hunt. The young man, his wife, and the brother-in-law sat huddled together in the front seat of their Ford pickup truck. The road was rough in places and they slowly made their way toward the old farm. The woods closed in on them from both sides traveling down the narrow dirt road. Something in the air was different tonight. They all felt it!

Ahead they saw the Englishman's old house. It was nearly covered from top to bottom with vines and a high growth of weeds choking any sign of flowers in the front yard. The three looked around them for assurance there was no game warden to be found. The young woman suddenly blurted out she smelled wood smoke. They all smelled the wood smoke as they got closer to the house. To their surprise they could see smoke coming from a chimney where nobody could possibly live. As they sat in wonder of it all, candlelights began to appear in the downstairs windows with shadows moving about. The three became frightened and started to leave when the sound of screams came seemingly from all around them. The young man threw the truck back into gear in an effort to escape the ghostly happenings. From behind them, they heard the thundering sound of horse's hooves striking hard against the road, coming straight for them.

The next day, they ventured back to the old house with several friends to find out what was happening. It was their opinion someone knew they were coming and tried to scare them. Upon reaching the deserted house, they had to force their way in. They found nothing. There were no old candles; the fireplace had not been used for a very long time. There were no ashes of any kind. They inspected the fireplace and found that if someone lit a fire it would have burned the house down. The dust and dirt lay thick on everything in sight and no sign of anybody having been there for years.

Was this the ghost of a man who came home to murder his family? The house still stands and would be dangerous to attempt entry. Some of the locals say you can still hear the horses and screams in the night. When you see the candles and smell the wood smoke, it is a wise man who turns the other way.

12

Cabarrus County

The very first gold mine ever to be found in the United States was discovered by Conrad Reed, the son of a Hessian soldier who deserted during the Revolutionary War. This one mine alone yielded enough gold that it warranted a mint to be opened for processing the fortune. The Reed Mine is now a historic landmark in Cabarrus County.

Nestled in the foothills of the Uwharrie Mountains, a trove of superstitions, ghosts, folklore, and tales of the supernatural abound here in Cabarrus. The Uwharrie Mountains have been called the most haunted mountains in the world.

The Hanging Tree

A blacksmith was much more than a luxury for centuries. When a horse was used for riding, pulling wagons, or plowing fields, it was discovered the odds of them becoming crippled from these uses lessened greatly if they were shod. The blacksmith plied his trade shoeing the animals, but a blacksmith was much more. If you needed anything made of iron, he was the artisan you went to see. He could repair the wheels of your wagon and carriages. The manufacture of farming and hand tools could also be done here. A vast majority of the iron work we specialize in now was all produced by one man, the blacksmith.

Every community did not have a resident blacksmith. Just as you had ministers that traveled from town to town, so did the average blacksmith. On the third Saturday of each month, John would come to a particular spot in the mountains of Wautauga County to ply his trade. He would make his camp beneath a huge old oak that produced enough shade for him to work and stay reasonably cool. People from the surrounding communities came to him for the things they needed. John would stay one week to make sure everyone had enough time to see him.

John was far from being a little man and his physical strength was to be admired. He held a good head for business and was easy to deal with. He believed in a fair price for his services and nobody ever complained. The quality of his work was always nothing but the best to be found.

In the summer of 1820, John set up his camp and unloaded his portable bellows. His tools were placed neatly on the back of the wagon and he was open for business. The people came and went, each happy with their purchases and vowed to see him again when he returned on his next trip. The great limbs of the ancient oak seemed to sigh in the wind. The sound was close to a whisper as John sat drinking water and enjoying his noonday meal.

Looking up, he saw three men riding toward him on the backs of mules. One of the mules walked as though he had a sore foot. John stood to his feet and watched as they finally reached his station. They greeted each other cordially and struck a bargain for John to replace a shoe on the mule. They watched John as he placed the money for the service in a large leather pouch in the back of the wagon. The three men inquired as to how much longer John would be in the area. They gave the reason for asking that they would have more work for him on Friday. John told them he would still be there until Saturday morning and then he was to leave for the journey home.

The three men left John and rode their mules slowly down the road out of sight. Later in the evening John was counting his money for the week and his thoughts began to wander. He had never seen these men here before and he thought he knew almost everybody and most of their children, but these were strangers. John decided he would hide his money. There was something about the strangers that John did not trust. One of the men wore a pistol in his belt. This was not unusual, but the way he carried himself was not the way of a man at peace. His gentle voice and kind words did not match the look in his eyes.

Friday came early for John; several farmers were waiting for him at almost the crack of dawn. The farmers were with him until noon. One of the strangers John had shod the mule for was riding up the road toward him. He rode slowly and nodded as he rode past. John asked the local farmers if they knew the man. None of the farmers had ever seen him before, but they all agreed he looked like trouble. They asked John if he wanted them to stay for awhile in case of trouble. John laughed lightly. "I can handle that kind of trouble. I appreciate your offer though." The farmers paid John and bid him good-bye. One of the old farmers had even brought John a fresh pie as a gift for being good to them over the years.

John knew he had a good week and his wife would be pleased at the amount of money he had brought home. Normally, there was just as much barter as cash, but this week was different. John assured himself his money was safely hidden from prying eyes and then sat down to eat his supper. As evening drew closer, John went to his wagon and pulled an old revolver wrapped in linen from under the seat. He assured himself it was loaded and returned to his seat beneath the old Oak. He placed his back against the tree so he could not be surprised from behind. His every nerve was on edge with the anticipation of robbers in his camp.

John was known to sleep lightly. On this night, though, he never heard a sound until the muzzle of a pistol was placed at his forehead. The three men had returned and demanded his money. John refused and tried to fight them. The three men were able to subdue the blacksmith in a short time. John's pistol lay at his feet useless to him. The robbers could not stay for long without fear of getting caught in the act. They retrieved a rope from the back of John's wagon and threw one end over one of the huge limbs of the oak tree. If he did not tell them where his money was, they were going to hang him. John never spoke of his money. This was known by the way the robbers had ransacked the entire camp. He did promise them that if he was hanged there would never be peace for any of them.

They hanged John and watched as he kicked and twitched at the end of his own rope. The three men did find the money and made their escape into the night. Two of the robbers were never seen again. The third was captured and tried for his crime two years later in Buncombe County. He was hanged for the murder and robbery of the blacksmith.

Through the years, travelers found the camp beneath the old oak to be a perfect resting place, but none of them were ever able to spend the night. The sound of a rope creaking on a limb above them was too unnerving! The shadow of a man hanging was seen on many occasions. In later years, the area was called the Devil's Trading Post. Sleeping beneath the shade of the tree many woke to find their personal items missing. Money from their pockets just disappeared! Looking about them, there was never any tracks other than their own to show someone had been there with them. Some say it is John returned from the dead. John was not a thief; even in death, he would have no reason to steal from strangers. Others prefer to believe it is the Devil himself continuing the trade of three violent men who killed an innocent man for the sake of his money.

The old oak is long gone now and the land was cleared for the building of a new home. The spot where the tree stood is part of a highway leading to the town of Boone. It is hoped John is resting in peace.

Who's There?

T he town of Hayesville was incorporated in 1913. The years before it became Hayesville, the site on which the town now sits was the Cherokee town of Quanassee. Located in Clay County, there is easy access to the states of Georgia and Tennessee with an entry to the Unicoi Mountain Range. Lake Chatuge, its scenic shoreline, holds secrets of the ages when men first came here to make their homes.

Small community churches were also used as meetinghouses in earlier times. People came from all over the area to vote on important matters or just to enjoy themselves with their neighbors. Other functions for the young at heart were barn dances. Local musicians gathered together and played their music for a small fee or just for the fun of it all.

Fire's Creek is now a part of Nantahala National Forest. It wasn't always that way. There were small farms and homes dotted throughout the mountains. The home of Wade P. and his family lay two miles from his church and a neighbor's barn everyone used for dances and parties. To travel to the church for Sunday services or community meetings, he would have to take a narrow road around the ford to the wooden bridge crossing the creek. This route was far longer than the path across the hollow. The short-cut through the hollow was much faster.

As the years passed, Wade became a young man who wanted to have his independence. There was to be a social gathering and barn dance on Saturday. He asked his parents for permission to attend. His father agreed to let him attend the social on one condition: "When you leave the barn, take the road home. Do not cross the hollow after dark." Wade never remembered his father crossing the hollow after dark in his entire life.

Wade followed his father's direction and kept to the road. After a few trips like this one, Wade wanted to hurry home and the path across the hollow looked very tempting. Each time he would attend a gathering or his family knew he would be coming home after dark, they would remind him not to travel through the hollow after dark.

It was not unusual for Wade's grandfather to visit for long periods of time during the warmer months of the year. On a pleasant Saturday afternoon, Wade bathed and dressed himself in his finest clothes. As he walked out onto the porch, his grandfather grinned. "I see by the way you're dressed, there must be a young lady you have your eye on."

Wade smiled broadly. "Yes, sir, and I hope she sees me the same way."

His grandfather's eyes twinkled in the afternoon light. "I still remember those days. When I saw your grandma, I thought she was the prettiest thing I had ever seen. Lord knows I never thought we would get married and have a house full."

Wade sat down beside his grandfather. "I have a question for you if you don't mind."

The old man's eyes narrowed slightly and nodded his head. The young man leaned forward, speaking in a low voice. "Everybody tells me not to cross the hollow after dark. It sure would make it a lot easier on me if I did. What is in the hollow they all seem to worry about?"

The old man shook his head. "The hollow has a ghost. It ain't a regular ghost. This one will come home with you and you don't have a choice in the matter. He will cause you and your family more trouble than you want to deal with. More than one has pushed their luck and wound up with something in the house that ain't right. You just stay away from there after dark and you'll be alright."

Wade nodded and then left for the barn dance. He returned at his usual time and did not cross the hollow. He decided to talk to his grandfather again about the ghost in the hollow and found out that his own family had been a victim to the ghostly visits. His grandfather told Wade he had crossed the hollow late one evening while coon hunting. For several weeks his life became a hell he never wanted to see again. He would not repeat what had happened. He gathered himself and left the porch headed for the well.

Wade did not believe in ghosts. He had crossed the hollow all his life in the daylight and never saw anything to fear. There was never a sign of bear or bobcat tracks and the fishing there was top-notch.

The evening wore on and Wade stepped from the barn looking up at the evening sky. Clouds had moved in and the smell of rain was in the air. Wade went back inside and bid his friends good-night. He said he was going home before the rain started. Leaving the barn dance he started up the road toward home. The further he walked he began to notice the rain clouds were becoming very dark and stormy looking. Wade decided on this night he would prefer taking the short-cut through the hollow and chance a ghost than being soaked in a pouring rain.

He had barely been on the path a few minutes when he thought he heard the voice of a man up ahead of him. Cautiously, he moved

This is the path through the hollow said to be the home of a spirit that likes to be appeased for trespassing on his land.

forward and saw not a soul, but the voice became louder. What the voice was saying was unintelligible, but plain to the ear. Deeper into the hollow, Wade heard the sound of footsteps almost dogging his tracks. The steps were heard with every step he took. He began to sweat profusely. Knowing there was someone in the hollow and not showing themselves made him nervous. Ahead Wade saw the opening for one of his father's fields and the end of the path. He had barely reached the end of the path when he felt as though he had been pushed from behind. He was pushed so hard he nearly fell on his face. He whirled in his tracks ready to fight! To his surprise, nobody was there — he was alone in the darkness.

The next morning, his father looked at him quizzically and asked, "Who were you in a fight with last night?"

Wade told him he had not been in a fight. This made his father angry because he thought Wade was lying to him.

"If you didn't get in a fight, then why is your face scratched up?"

Wade had no idea he had even the slightest scratch and sat in amazement at his father's words. His grandfather never looked up from his plate. "I think you took the path through the hollow last night."

Knowing he would be in trouble, Wade lied to his father. "No, I might have gotten the scratches when I fell in the yard last night. It was pretty dark and I tripped." Both of the men dropped the subject and continued on with their day.

Wade retired to his room shortly after dark. He had worked hard that day and he was ready for sleep. Shortly before midnight. Wade woke shivering in his bed. The covers lay in a heap near the end of the bed. Reaching down, he grabbed the covers and tried to pull them up. They barely budged. He assumed they must be caught on the corner of the bed somehow. Getting up, he grabbed the sheets and tugged. They gave way easily and he tried to put them back on the bed. They were suddenly wrenched from his hands and sailed across the room landing by the bedroom door. Wade stood amazed and thought he had been dreaming. Carefully, he picked up the bed covers and lay back on his bed.

Wade and his father worked in the barn for most of the morning, cleaning and repairing stalls. The entire morning his father kept looking at him as though something was on his mind. When lunch time came, they talked about what was on his father's mind. Wade had to try and explain why it had sounded like he was herding cattle in his room late the night before. The answer was just another lie for Wade to live with. He told his father he had fallen while sleepwalking. His father's humor never ceased to amaze him. He told Wade to sleepwalk a little quieter so he and Wade's mother could sleep.

For nearly another month Wade was cursed with a ghost that had followed him home from the hollow. He heard laughter in his room late in the night from a disembodied voice. He was constantly being touched or pushed from behind. Each time he would close his eyes to sleep, something woke him. When he could bear it no longer, he approached his grandfather and told him what he had done. Wade also told him what was happening to him during the night while he tried to sleep. His grandfather listened patiently and let him finish his story.

His grandfather then sat down by a tree close to the barn in the shade from the afternoon sun. "Sit down here, boy, and I'll tell you a story. When I was a young man like yourself, I used to take the short-cut through the hollow on the way over to the mill. Just like you, I was a little bullheaded and didn't believe what folks told me.

"The ground you are sittin' on right now used to belong to the Indians. That hollow over there...it was theirs, too. If I remember right, my Daddy told me about an old Indian that refused to leave this land when the soldiers came in to take them all away. He put up a fight and killed a bunch of them. Eventually, they killed him and dragged his body out there somewhere and buried him. The old folks tell it that he never left the hollow. His ghost still lives there and the land is still his.

"He don't bother nobody...less they come through there at night. Sometimes he will follow you home just to let you know you trespassed on his land and made him mad. I knew where you'd been the morning when I saw your face. By then, it was already too late to remind you of what you done. The only way you're going to get rid of this Indian is tell him you're sorry and leave some tobacco for a gift on the stump by the creek. It usually works pretty good."

As the old man said this, he winked at his grandson. "That was the way I got rid of him anyway. I stayed away from that hollow ever since."

Wade went to the store the next morning and purchased a small bag of pipe tobacco. On his return, he stopped at the stump by the creek and placed the bag on top. He asked the Indian for forgiveness and promised he would never again cross the hollow at night, disturbing his rest. He felt better after doing so, but felt as though someone was watching him the entire time he was in the hollow.

Wade was never bothered again by the ghost from the hollow and he learned a valuable lesson. Later in life, he married and made his home near Franklin, North Carolina. His children have been told the story many times just to be made aware that folktales are not always something to pass the time. In the hollow, the Indian may still be watching for those who dare to intrude upon his home. A gift of friendship may be a good thing to leave for him if you decide you want to cross his land. Yes, the old stump is still there by the creek waiting for your gifts of peace.

13

Burke County

In 1567, the Spanish made an attempt to place a colony here. Captain Juan Pardo built a fort and claimed the land for the Colony of Spanish Florida. Fort San Juan was occupied by thirty soldiers when Captain Pardo left the fort and continued his exploration. In 1568, the Native Americans attacked, killing the Spanish and burning the fort. There was not another attempt to colonize the area until two hundred years later when the Europeans arrived.

Burke County was the center for the largest Native American settlement in North Carolina. The settlement for these mound builders dated back as far as 1000 AD expanding over centuries.

The Brown Mountain Lights

Western North Carolina stories are never complete without the tale of the Brown Mountain lights. Ten miles north of Morganton is a U-shaped mountain with a high peak visible at one end. The Brown Mountain lights are elusive. There are long periods of time when they cannot be seen. If you are fortunate and do get to witness this phenomena, you will see anywhere from ten to hundreds of lights bouncing and flickering among the trees of the mountaintop.

The Cherokee and the Catawba Indians reported seeing the Brown Mountain lights long before the first written report was ever published around 1850. The story of these lights can be found in much of their lore, both written and oral.

Out of the many stories of those trying to explain why these lights exist, the most popular seems to be of a great battle. The Cherokee and the Catawba went to war in about the year 1200. The battle lasted for many days and nights. It is believed the lights of Brown Mountain are the ghost lights of torches where the battle raged. Some believe it is the torches of the Cherokee women searching for their dead warriors.

Popular among the romantics is the story of a young woman who lost her lover on this mountain and the torches from the men of the community can still be seen searching for him in the night. His body was never found.

The third, and most heard, story is that of a young man who lived close by Brown Mountain. He became unfaithful to his wife and wanted her out of his life. She still loved him regardless of his abuse and refused to leave him. He continued his love affair and made plans to rid himself of his wife once and for all. During this time, she became pregnant with his child. This did not deter his plans to be rid of her.

One night his temper could not be contained. In a fit of rage, he killed his wife and buried her on Brown Mountain. He never thought anybody would ever find where she was buried. After his foul deed was done, he went back to his cabin and made his plans to leave. Before morning, he slipped away into the night and was never seen again.

Neighbors went to the Sheriff, worried about the woman. They had known of her being abused and worried for her safety when she did not come into town. The law found dried blood inside the empty cabin and began a search of the area. They found no sign of the woman or her husband. The search lasted for weeks. When they felt the search was in vain, a fresh grave was discovered. The grave contained the remains of a young woman and the skull of a baby. So the tale goes that the lights are torches searching for the woman who was viciously murdered by her husband.

For more than two hundred years, laymen and scientists have researched the lights in an effort to explain them. Some of the most fascinating theories are from those who have never delved into the history of the lights. Skeptics have announced the lights are reflections of automobile headlights coming through the trees of the mountains or bouncing off rocks. This does not have any rhyme or reason, considering the lights were witnessed over one hundred years before the invention of the automobile. There wasn't even a road during this period of time.

A U.S. Geological study made a fantastic discovery around 1913. According to their experts, the Brown Mountain lights were the reflection of the light on a train passing through the mountains. Where the problem lies with this expert opinion is the simple historical fact that a flood one year before completely destroyed the railroad tracks. There were no trains running at that time, so the lights could not have been from a locomotive. Also, a single train cannot reflect lights — hundreds of lights — at a distance of ten miles!

The lights are accused of being anything from foxfire to swamp gas. The real reason is still unknown and defies explanation. A little known fact for those having an avid interest in geology, Brown Mountain sits on top of a fault line called The Grandfather Mountain Fault. Lights such as these have been seen over mountains that are located on a fault and were seen before Mount Saint Helen's eruption. After the eruption, the lights were never seen again.

Being the romantic that I am, I prefer to believe the story of a historic battle between the Catawba and the Cherokee, but the mystery continues!

14

Henderson County

During the Civil War, Henderson County served the Confederacy with 1,296 troops. It also served the Union with 130 troops. This all culminated from a total population of almost 10,000 people. Connemara was the final home of Carl Sandburg. The famous Woodfield Inn, built in 1852, became the home of all the Confederate soldiers when they were not on the battlefield.

Henderson County counts upon its legends as being host to one of the most infamous haunts in North Carolina. It is the John Drew House. The house is no longer standing, but the legends and superstitions are still respected for many parts of this county.

Only Superstition

So many people have watched as someone at the dinner table knocked over the salt shaker, spilling salt. They immediately get a pinch of the salt and pitch it over their left shoulder. After all "They" say it will ward off bad luck.

Through the years, all of us have tried to figure out who "They" are. Was it someone of the scientific community or was it the old woman down the road? The truth is we have not the slightest idea. However, here are a few of the rules "They" say to live by.

- At dinner, it is rude to take the last slice of bread, but, beware, if you take bread and already have bread, it is the sign of company coming to see you. You must never turn a loaf of bread upside down after a slice is removed from it. Your luck will surely go sour.

- There are things you need to protect your home from lightning strikes. It is very simple: You should place an acorn on your window sill.

- If you wear your best beads and you have children, they should be amber. This will prevent illness and is said to cure colds. A serious condition such as croup in children is easily remedied by passing a live chicken over the child's head.

- A dinner bell was used in a time long past to call the family in for dinner... This bell has another function not to be forgotten: If you ring the bell, it will drive demons away from your home. It is said they hate the noise of the bell. For more protection from evil, also wear a blue bead. It will protect you from witches.

- Death brings many warnings to a house when a loved one or friend has passed. All mirrors should be covered that are in the room with the deceased. This is to prevent him or her from seeing themselves and transferring their spirit into the mirror only to take over the body of the next person who looks into the mirror. The dead can steal your soul if you look into their eyes. Was there a warning before your loved one passed?

A bird in the house is a warning of a death in the home. When you bury those you love, there should always be a tombstone — it keeps the dead from rising. The carving of someone's name on the tombstone will assure eternal rest. If your loved one died on Good Friday, he is assured a place in heaven.

- Everyone loves to look their very best. One of the ways we groom ourselves is by cutting our hair. If you cut your hair on Good Friday, you will not have headaches for the rest of the year. For better luck, do not cut your fingernails on Friday or Sunday or your luck is sure to fail you. Further assurance in good luck for the coming year is for you to wear new clothes on Easter Sunday.

- The proverbial black cat is said to bring some bad luck. This is true... unless the cat is walking toward you. Need that good luck reversed, just take a stroll beneath a ladder and your bad luck will be back.

- If you catch a leaf falling from a tree in the autumn, you will not catch a cold all winter. For more serious conditions, you should wear the dried body of a frog in a silk bag around your neck. It will rid you of epilepsy and other fits.

- Mothers are a very special breed of humanity. They endure the very things men will not attempt to try and control. A new mother giving birth should have a sharp knife placed beneath her bed. It will ease the pains of labor and make for a smoother birth of the child.

- Dreams enter our lives on a regular basis as we sleep. Scientists say we dream the most just before our waking state, though it sometimes seems as if we dreamt the whole night. We all wonder what the dream means when it seems unusual to us. To dream of angels means success and happiness in your life. There are also dreams of animals, such as cats; these dreams are usually unfortunate, for they mean treachery in your life. If the cat attacks you, it is said you have enemies. However, a dream of someone visiting you who is known to be dead is generally a good omen. They are bearers of messages from beyond and have come to advise you. Heed their words well.

The thousands of superstitions that have been handed down through the centuries come from many sources. The Europeans brought superstitions to America that are still very much in practice today, passed among us with few knowing where or when these particular practices began. These superstitions are especially deeply ingrained in the modern practices of funeral rites: the covering of the mirrors, the assurance that the eyes are closed, and, most of all, a properly marked gravesite. One small thought has crossed many minds. The latches on the coffin open from the outside only. Is that for our protection? Just a passing thought.

15

Avery County

Well known for its high concentration of quartz, Avery County, tucked away in the mountains of Western North Carolina, is a Mecca for tourists from all over the world. The county was formed in 1911 and was named after yet another Revolutionary War soldier, Colonel Waightstill Avery.

Avery County's claim to fame is their Christmas tree harvest and the undying pride and loyalty to their ancestors and their country. Avery was the last county created in North Carolina, though it was well established in the early 1700s.

Mystery in the Black

Proof of habitation in the Black Mountains during the years 8000 through 1000 BC have been discovered by archeologists. They know for certain the American Indian lived and hunted here long before the Europeans knew of their existence. The Black Mountains of North Carolina are easily found east of Asheville. Joara was a native village where it was said Hernando de Soto spent time during his expedition here. The Juan Pardo Expedition was also thought to have spent much time in the village of Joara, close by Swannanoa Gap, in 1567.

There is much to be said of their encounters with the American Indian. The Spaniards were sure to have learned some of the mysteries of the mountains surrounding them. There lies the highest mountain peak in North Carolina named Mount Mitchell. When the Spanish ventured into this land, it was called simply The Black Mountains for no other reason than the impression it gave from a distance.

In 1785, the eastern fringe of the Black Mountains was hunting lands for the Cherokee. The land was signed away with all rights to the United States, and the Europeans began to move into the territory, measuring and renaming these peaks and valleys for their own.

For the men of the expeditions, they were amazed to find balds on these peaks and mountaintops where nothing would grow. There was nothing wrong with the soil on these balds. In most cases, the soil on the bald was far richer than the soil around it, growing trees at even higher elevations. The Indians knew the reason: these were sacred places where you had to respect the being that came to stay or visit. Some of the balds were forbidden to everyone and were used only for burial purposes.

The balds are considered to be where the four winds of the spirits meet. The Europeans, as well as the Spanish soldiers, despite having their own superstitions, completely disregarded the information the Cherokee had provided to them. At times, the Cherokee were admonished for daring to attempt to hold back the strangers from going to places that were considered dangerous for them to be.

As the seasons made themselves known by the turning of the leaves on the trees, the leaves of red, gold, orange, and brown turned the mountains into a land of unparalleled beauty. It was a time of harvest for the Cherokee and most warriors were unavailable to the Europeans for guiding them through the mountains. A hunting party comprised of German immigrants made plans to journey into the wilderness near Grandfather Mountain. They had heard of the bounty of game to be had there and wanted the meat to store for the winter months ahead. The Cherokee elders advised them this was not a time for them to go to the mountain. They were told to wait until the second moon of the harvest and it would be safe, but the hunting party dismissed the elders of the tribe and left their homes in search of food for the winter.

Days passed and there was no word from the hunters. The families asked the Cherokee if they would search for them because they knew the Black Mountains better than anyone. The Cherokee elders refused to allow any of the Cherokee to help with the search for the men. He told them again they must wait for the second moon of the harvest when it was safe. The immigrants' families asked the elders what was the danger? The elders told them, "The spirit of the Bear and the Deer danced and prayed for his people during the time of harvest so all may be well in the winter. The spirit of the Cherokee warriors who walked the path before would come back to the rock of the four winds to give thanks to the Father. This is a time when you cannot see them. It is forbidden. The Father has given us this law and we have always obeyed his words. We will speak of this no more until the second moon is high and the harvest is done."

With these words, the elders turned their backs on the settlers and continued the harvest. The settlers were angry and promised the Cherokee if they did not help them they would destroy their village. One night later, the elders met to discuss what they were to do in order to prevent the settlers from destroying their village as well as angering the Father. It was decided two warriors would

The bald where several hunters disappeared without a trace. Note: This is private property and cannot be accessed without permission of the owner.

take the search party deep into the mountains, but would not enter the land of the spirits.

The settlers assembled and followed the Cherokee. The Indians found tracks of the White men headed for Grandfather Mountain. They tracked the men for two days and stopped near a peak covered in fir trees. The Cherokee pointed toward a high peak and told them they should start to look for their friends on the other side. It was obvious to the Cherokee where the hunting party had gone, but they were not about to go any further with fear of reprisal from the elders.

Reaching the summit, the settlers began to journey down the other side over the jagged rocks continuing the search into Avery County. From the plateau, the Cherokee watched as the men crossed the valley and began the climb toward the bald until they were out of sight.

The Cherokee waited two more days and were preparing to return home when the search party was sighted again. The men moved slowly and within a day they were back among the Cherokee. The warriors never spoke as they kept moving toward their village. When it was time to camp, the warriors made their camp away from the White men and refused to speak with them. The Cherokee did not want to take the chance that the White men had angered the spirits and would take revenge on them.

It was no surprise to the Indians the hunting party was not to be found. What had happened to them brought them no sorrow because they had been warned not to desecrate sacred land by their presence. The search party, looking haggard and bewildered from what they had discovered, reported to the rest of the settlement what they had seen and heard.

"We convinced the Cherokee to take us as far as Grandfather Mountain, but they would not go any further. The rest of us continued over the mountain and passed through the valley until we reached the falls. To the west, we saw a bald with what seemed to be some smoke rising from a small fire. We headed for the bald and arrived there the next day early in the afternoon. During the night, we could plainly see the light of a fire coming from the bald.

"We climbed from the North Slope to reach the bald hoping everything was well in the camp. This was not the case. We found where they had built lean-tos for shelter. The fire coals were still hot to the touch. Our friends were nowhere to be found! The tracks from their boots stopped and disappeared into nothing as if they had been taken off the Earth. All the rifles and food were still there and a pipe belonging to someone was found still hot enough to light a match from its bowl. We searched the area and could not find them. We called their names and each man answered. The problem was they all sounded like they were far away and the voices came from above us toward the treetops. We heard the growl of bears very close by and never found a track. The hunters were not there and we never found them!"

The town reorganized another search party and returned to the abandoned camp on the bald. They brought back everything they found and returned the items to the families. Neither the hunters nor their bodies were ever discovered. Though the settlers tried to accuse the Cherokee of killing them, the leader of the settler's town advised them against this for fear of war between the tribes and their own people.

When tensions began to ease between the two settlements, the elders came to visit the leaders to try and explain to them what had happened to the men. "It is as we have told you. It was a time for the spirits, not a time for men. The hunters were not killed as you may think. Your hunters came to the sacred place where the four winds meet. You will never find these men. They have been taken by the spirits." With this being said, the elders walked away, never to return to the settlement for what they had done.

It does not matter what we believe or disbelieve, but these hunters disappeared as though they never existed. Did the spirits seek revenge for their intrusion upon them? The Cherokee say yes. The settlers of the time still cannot fathom what could have happened to the men. There are things in this world we were just not meant to understand.

16

Buncombe County

T hough the history of Buncombe County is grand, it still stands in the shadows today. The shadow was created by George Vanderbilt and his 250-room mansion that receives about one million visitors a year. The estate is 125 acres, of which seventy-five are gardens and museums for the world to enjoy.

In 1791, Buncombe County was called a state because of the amount of land within its boundaries. The English, Scottish, and the Germans inhabited the county during the mid 1700s. Thomas Wolfe, Zebulon B. Vance, and David L. Swain were just a few of the prominent and well-respected names of men who were natives of Buncombe County.

Battle Mansion

The year 2006 brought the end of an era for Battle Mansion. It was located close to the Grove Park Inn, which has become known for its legend of being haunted, and became home for WLOS television until it was torn down to make way for condominiums.

The estate was originally built as a private residence by Dr. Samuel Battle and has gone through many changes since its construction in 1928. The Historic Preservation Society of Asheville had wanted to designate the structure as a historic site. The problem lay in too many changes had been made and the cost of restoring it to its original condition was a price nobody wanted to pay for tax reasons.

The stone structure was magnificent in its own way. Those who were familiar with the building also knew of its visitors from beyond. When the original owners occupied the residence, a young servant girl was either pushed or fell down the stairs. Employees and visitors claim to have seen the young servant on occasion always wearing the same clothing. They all described her as wearing a long, old-fashioned dress. None of the descriptions ever noted the color of the dress or any facial features. History has yet to tell us the name of this young lady or why she may be haunting the property. Was she so unimportant to society that all have forgotten her name? We would like to think not.

Dr. Battle was a man of stature in his community. During the years of his life, Asheville society was anything but neutral. The list of the rich and famous people who came to stay in this fair city is long and very impressive. The Vanderbilts alone made history with its guests from around the world. Samuel Battle was deeply imbedded in the cream of this society. He attended the plays and concerts. His face was familiar at most, if not all, formal affairs in the area. With this in mind, we have no doubt the man seen in formal attire haunting the house was Samuel Battle. A former maintenance worker attested to seeing a man in formal attire in the house and identified Samuel Battle as the apparition he had seen from a picture presented to him.

Other employees have had their share of experiences. Witnesses say they have seen wires hanging from the ceiling and were moving on their own accord. One employee left the area as quickly as possible and swore someone unseen grabbed him.

Is this legend or fact? An official investigation was never founded as far as my research has been able to find. A scientific inquiry would have possibly answered many questions. The same young lady who was said to have been the servant of the Battle family has also been seen on the Grove Park property. Coincidence? You would never know unless you knew the history behind the young lady's services. It may have been possible she secured jobs at both the Inn and service in the home of Dr. Battle.

In this case, the sightings have never been proven or unproven and now can never be decided. It is for the romantic to believe a man such as Dr. Battle would return to his home and dress accordingly for the occasion. One must look his best when he is entertaining his guests. The servant who lost her life on the stairs may be rendering a heartfelt plea to the living to help her in her plight. Obviously she died before she was ready and makes herself known to others in an effort to stay among us.

It is usually known that where you have one occurrence there are more that have never been told for fear of being mocked. Are there more than one specter walking the halls? I would tend to believe so with the tales of people being grabbed while trying to tend to their work.

The story of Battle Mansion is not to be left to rest with just this writing. We are in hopes of more evidence and a more detailed history may be brought forth to try and solve a mystery. It is always pleasant to find a legend is more than a legend and the facts are found to echo their truth through time immortal.

Index

About the Author

Micheal served as a United States Marine during Vietnam. A native North Carolinian, he furthered his education in Chicago, Illinois, and colleges in North Carolina. While living in Chicago, he served the community as an Emergency Medical Technician.

Micheal has more than thirty years experience investigating and collecting stories of the paranormal, and was the recipient of an Editor's Choice award for some of his previous writings. His first release was the novel *Voyage of the Black Witch*. His newest release is *Ghosts of the North Carolina Shores*, published by Schiffer Publishing, Ltd.

Micheal currently resides in Whittier, North Carolina, and is the lead investigator for the Smoky Mountain Ghost Trackers of Western North Carolina. They continue to investigate areas reported to have paranormal activity and report their findings for evidence of spiritual activity. Visit his Facebook page at Smokey Mountain Ghost Trackers. You may also contact Micheal at www.michealrivers.com.